T0354584

PROFITS

—— IN ——

REAL ESTATE

RENTALS

DOUBLE YOUR INCOME
WITH SHORT TERM RENTALS

EVELINA MANNARINO

Order this book online at www.trafford.com
or email orders@trafford.com

Most Trafford titles are also available at major online book retailers.

Printed in the United States of America.

ISBN: 978-1-4669-7020-5 (sc)
ISBN: 978-1-4669-7019-9 (e)

Trafford rev. 12/12/2012

 www.trafford.com

North America & international
toll-free: 1 888 232 4444 (USA & Canada)
phone: 250 383 6864 ♦ fax: 812 355 4082

TABLE OF CONTENTS

Attitude of Gratitude

Of course no project is complete without the help of other people involved. People come in and out of our lives at a precise time for a specific reason.

I attended a free Raymond Aaron seminar in Edmonton in 2011. One of his ideas was to write a book to promote your company. Although I didn't make it to the last day of the seminar, I did remember that the seminar was about writing a book. So, thank you Raymond Aaron for the idea!

My sister, Julene has been a great inspiration! She checked in with me every week to see how I was doing and kept encouraging me to keep going and finishing this book. She supports me in everything I do and is a constant inspiration to me. Thank you, Julene!

My husband has always supported me with his "don't bother" attitude. That always fuels me to get it done! This book has been in my computer for about a year now until he told me to get a job, apart from being a full time stay at home mother. So, thank you hunny. If it weren't for you, this book would still be sitting in my computer! I love you, my husband.

I appreciate the help I received from Don Campbell, owner of the Real Estate Investment Network. As busy as this man is, he took time out of his monthly seminar to help me with how to write a book on real estate. He has thousands of people demanding his attention but still got back to me about a question that I had. I was very surprised that he remembered I had a question but very thrilled that he took the time to research my question and get back to me. I was very impressed. Thank you, Mr. Campbell!

My sister Fawn has always been a great motivator. Through our ups and downs and our matter of fact advice to each other, we make it through thick and thin. What kind of sisters would we be if we didn't throw something at each other every once in a while?

Drew, my friend and fellow author and has always answered thousands of questions that I had about writing a book. He answered all of them and has given me endless advice and help. Thanks so much, Drew and best wishes with Grecko the Gecko!

Most importantly are my little darlings. Tyson is my little man whom I am always proud of. I love you, big guy! My little baby princess: she makes writing a book challenging with her squealing, drooling and hair pulling. Love you and your big, brown eyes and huge smile.

A huge thank you to you: the reader. I appreciate you taking the time to purchase and read the book. I hope you enjoy it, learn something from it and most importantly, profit from it. Thanks again!

CHAPTER 1

Real Estate:
The Best Long Term Investment

Real estate investments are by far the safest and most secure investments out there, in my opinion. Yes, they may be slow and boring at times and you generally don't double or triple your income over night like the stock market can, however, you can sleep at night knowing that it's going to be there when you wake up.

During times like this when the economy is not at its best, there are still some good things about it. Real estate is like most business cycles—it has its ups and it has its downs. Just like a stock market, it's a good idea to purchase when the prices are low and sell them when they are high. Your specific goals and plans in real estate will determine where and when you make your purchases. Some people like to purchase and hold for the long term. I personally like to buy and never sell unless the transaction will make a huge difference in my portfolio. If I have one property where the value is going down, cash flow is very poor and it's hard to rent, then I may consider selling that one if I can exchange it for a property that will gain in value and have positive cash flow as well as being an easy money maker. Then, I would go ahead and sell one for another one.

The approach with long-term investing is that you should expect to make money in three ways when owning this property. You will make money without doing anything when the property goes up in value over the years. You will also make money when your tenants pay down your mortgage, in turn, increasing your equity in that house. You will also make the extra cash flow every month when your rental income is higher than your monthly bills. I personally like to take this extra cash flow and add it to my principle so that the mortgage gets paid down faster. I save interest and have more equity to play with in case I want to pull some money out for another property.

In this day and age where most people are not having a good time financially, instead of bragging how well you are doing, let's just join them for now. I don't mean be poor, I mean let's just act as if we don't have the extra cash at the end of the month. All the extra money we will put away so that we have money for a down payment on another house or pay down those mortgages so that when those interest rates finally do go up, it won't affect us as much.

Most people got in trouble because they were spending much more than they were earning. Don't get me wrong, I too am guilty of that. I did not need a Maserati Quattroporte, a Cadillac Escalade and a Toyota Matrix. Not only was the Toyota Matrix paid off, it was great on gas, had low insurance costs and the best part of all, it never went into the shop other than its routine oil change! However, I guess I needed the world to know how well I was doing and now I can join the rest too. I suggest, before making any big, spontaneous purchases, read a Dalai Lama book and get past the material possessions. This will not put you on towards a comfy retirement. Of course, I believe in rewarding yourself and those luxuries in life are made for all of us to share and use. One day, you can drive whatever you want but in the meantime, let's make some huge goals and make sure that you have your tenants making your Ferrari payments, not your positive cash flow.

With this uncertain economy, I also don't want you to rely on any old-age security payments, government pensions, your company pensions, etc. As we have all seen, companies go bankrupt. These are huge companies that no one would think would ever go down. If those big ones go down, yours may as well. That pension is not guaranteed, not matter what anyone tells you. Government pensions are not set in stone and these could change any day. You have noticed that some countries have changed their pension age as well so those people now have to work extra years to receive that pension. What about if we don't even make it to 67 years old? Even if we did, I don't know about you but I do not want to wake up when I'm 66 years old and have to go to work. Life is too short to spend this much time working towards a pension. I'm sorry, but a leaky toilet in the middle of the night sounds much better if I can retire at 50 or 60 at the latest. You must worry about this today, not tomorrow. And if I'm wrong, sorry, you'll just end with a couple of paid-off houses giving you a much higher monthly income than the government pension. I'm sure you will still forgive me then.

I got into an argument with my mother-in-law the other day. Well, she's Italian, so it's not an argument. They just talk and yell very loud so it seems like an argument but we are just talking. You have to know Italians to know what I'm talking about. She is a 65-year-old woman trying to convince me that my husband and I need to be paying into the CPP (Canadian Pension Plan) so that we can get that when we are older, otherwise we will be left with nothing. I was explaining to her that I don't trust the government or trust that the plan will be there when I retire.

"It's guaranteed!" She yells back.

"It's not guaranteed, nothing is guaranteed." I tell her. "If I have to put away $100 towards the CPP until I retire, then that's $38,400 when I retire. Now they have moved the age of retirement up to 67 and I am definitely not going to be working until I am 67 years old. My husband and I definitely want to retire much sooner than that. I would rather put that money away towards my mortgage and get that paid down so that when we do retire, and much sooner than 67, we can live off the rental income instead. I doubt that the CPP money we receive will even pay for our lifestyle that we enjoy. The only guarantee is that I will have a paid-off house when I retire." I thought I convinced her for sure.

"No, it's guaranteed, it's the government!" She insists.

Okay, well I am not going to argue. I am absolutely terrified if all I had to count on was the government to get me through my retirement years. I also don't want just enough for living expenses. My husband and I both want to have homes in Canada and Italy and be able to get up and get on a plane and go anywhere in the world at anytime. I doubt that anyone is living off a government pension and jet setting around the world. That is what we want and that is what we are working towards. We can only count on ourselves for that, not the CPP!

With the new and increased age of retirement, the government is now hoping that we lose extra seniors from the age between 65 and 67. A few seniors will not make it and this plan is strictly for financial reasons. The first one is that the seniors in that age bracket will have to contribute for an extra two years. Also in that same time frame, we will lose a few seniors. Mathematically, the government gains two years' worth of payments as well as loses a certain amount of seniors that they no longer have to pay out. Do you seriously want to work until you are 67? Really? And for what? A measly pension?

Although real estate investments can be tricky, I've had a few challenges myself. You cannot give up. You must keep talking to people until you find one that can explain everything in a way that does make it sound easy. It's not that difficult at all, just find the right person that will work with you and find something to invest in. That investment vehicle will make all the difference in your retirement years. An extra $1,000 or $2,000 is pretty good compared to receiving only a couple of hundred a month from the government. Not only that but you always have the option of selling the entire house in case a major expense comes up that the "government" would otherwise not give you money for. Or, you have the option of taking out a line of credit and have both the extra cash as well as the cash flow. You will need choices and options and you will want to be in control of your own finances. Counting on the government with no backup is absolutely terrifying and I don't know how anyone can sleep at night with that as the only option.

After my argument, I mean, talk, with my mother in law, I ended up "talking" with my sister in law. There was no yelling as she is not Italian, so it really was just a discussion. She just got a job at a bank and is pushing RRSP's as a great retirement option. Again, this is for the government to help themselves, not to help you. The more they get you to save your own retirement money, the less money they will have to give you in the end. I look at it as a clue: the government is telling you to save your money! They give you incentives today to do this as if they already know that the Canadian Pension Plan and other government plans won't be there. They are already encouraging you to save! To me, that is a big clue.

My other favorite part about that is that although you don't have to pay taxes on that today, they will certainly be taking their share of the taxes when you retire. Either way, they are getting your money, not saving you money. Their main incentive is that you have your own savings for retirement so that they are not feeling obligated to pay you. By the time you retire, the rules will have changed again and if you have saved up a certain amount, they will give you even less. You really can't win with them and again, they have all the control and make up all the rules.

In my personal opinion, I prefer owning a house instead of stocks. Stocks have the possibility to be worth absolutely nothing overnight or over a short period of time. You can lose all of your money without any control over it and without the option of ever making that back, no matter how long you wait it out. Once a company is gone, it's gone and it is not coming back. Worst case scenario with a house, let's say it burned to the ground and you didn't even have it insured. It is still worth something! No matter what, even if it blew up overnight, that property is still worth something. It will not be worth zero, ever. Yes, you would be in a bad spot, of course, but your investment will never become completely worthless as is possible with the stock market.

Yes, I do hear about those people that lost half their money in real estate. How did they calculate that? Let me tell you a little story here. I have my Toyota Matrix worth about $5,000. I go out one day and someone offers me $6,000 so I think about it. I then have someone offer me $7,000 for the same car. Wow, this is exciting, I didn't know my car was actually worth $7,000! He said that his friend just bought one for $7,000 and he wants the same one. I am definitely selling this car for $7,000 because I didn't know it was worth that much. So we agree and I'm waiting for the guy to show up with a check. No one shows up. I can't even get a hold of the guy who offered me the $6,000. Obviously, if that other guy sold that car for $7,000, plus mine is in better condition, then my car is definitely worth $7,000 and that other guy is getting a super deal if he shows up with $6,000. No one does show up. I go to bed that night being upset how I lost $2,000 that day.

The same story is happening with people's homes who claim that their homes are worth half of what they were worth last year. The truth is, your home was never worth that much to begin with. Yes, a couple of those houses sold for that much but they were never worth that. If you purchased that house for the highest price last year then yes, you can claim that your house is worth half of what you paid for it. Most people had that same house for many years, paid about $100,000, they think their house was worth $250,000 last year and are now depressed because their house is only worth $125,000 and think they lost half their money. The truth is, you made money—your house is worth $25,000 more than what you paid for it. In fact, you probably didn't put down more than $25,000 of your own cash, probably even much less. So, if you put down $25,000 on that $100,000 house and its now worth $125,000 then you have already doubled your money. No reason to be upset, it was never worth more than that anyways. Be happy that you have doubled your down payment.

Everyone should have at least one investment property in their portfolio for their retirement. I don't believe in RRSP's too much or any other form of government retirement savings. This is the government's way of asking you to save your own money because they probably will have none to give you anyway. You are giving them control of your savings which, in turn, they will distribute to you as they see fit. They will see how it fits in with social security, see how much you have and if you saved a lot, probably trim down what they will give you. This doesn't sound like too much fun for me.

If you own a piece of real estate, it will work alongside you while you work. You won't need to put too much money into it, certainly not as much as RRSP's or other retirement savings. Actually, if done correctly, it will give YOU money every single month. Can your other forms of savings do that? Realistically, you should have a house paid off in no more than 20 years. This would mean that there is no reason why you shouldn't have two, fully paid off houses before you retire. Also, look at the monthly income it brings in now. I like to count my houses and then multiply by the average income it brings in and then I will know what my retirement income looks like. For example, if I have 5 houses that bring in an average of $2,000 per month, once paid off, I should be receiving about $10,000 per month when I retire. I don't think that the government pension pays that much or any social security. I wouldn't know because I haven't looked because I simply don't care. I am focused on acquiring my properties, paying them off and knowing that I will be well taken care of. This gives me the option of retiring at any point in time if I choose to give up early and pay off one house with the equity from the other houses.

I love real estate so much that I can't see myself doing anything else. Even if I'm retired, I will probably still be buying houses and renting them out. I just love watching the money grow, I'm fascinated by it. I wonder how many I will end up with one day. I strongly urge you to have a backup plan in case your company goes bankrupt and there is no company pension or any other old age security payments from the government. Count on yourself first and if those people send you a check every month, well that is a bonus! You can use it to put gas in the Ferrari!

Now that we are ready to purchase something, get going on our own investments and take full control, let's look at the different ways of generating income with your property. There is the traditional way of putting a tenant in a home and hoping that they stay there for several years, which does work depending on the type of home you have.

Home Stays (international students)

You can also rent out the extra room that you have at your home to students, as room and board. Many companies offer services of placing students in homes and it is a good monthly rent. International students that come for a month or six weeks are a great way to learn about other cultures. Usually they are students under the age of 18 and in turn, they offer a really good monthly rate. The terms are from 6 weeks up to a full year. You are to take the students in and treat them like your own family so that they can learn the language and culture. These placement companies offer really good rates, you get a nice extra monthly income and a wonderful experience.

Renting Out Extra Rooms

Some holiday rental services offer placements for people that are looking to rent a room for a short time. This is like having a roommate but could be as short as overnight to several weeks. Most of these people are new to the area, need to save on accommodations and rather not stay alone. This way, they can learn about the new city, have a new friend in town and save on hotels. If you have an extra bedroom, why not rent it out for a couple of nights per week?

Another great idea with renting out rooms is that you can rent out your entire home or apartment while you are away on your own holidays. Not only will this pay for your accommodations elsewhere but you also have someone staying at your place while you are away. This is not a match made in heaven though. It is extremely important to ensure that you know who you have in there and can trust them. Perhaps have a neighbor or a friend check up on your place as well.

I have heard of an incident where the guests robbed the entire condo while the owner was away. They were in constant contact, the guests always replied to the owner's phone calls and emails however, they were moving out her items while they were staying at her place. Take every precaution necessary.

Home Exchange

A fantastic way to get free accommodations while you are on your holidays is to swap your place for someone else's. Although you won't make any money on this transaction, you will at least get to stay somewhere else for free. This method is becoming quite popular and you end up making really good friends as well. Of course, take every pre caution necessary as you don't want to end up with nowhere to stay but have already given your keys to some one else.

Long Term Rentals (Leases)

Long term rentals are great when you get a long term tenant in there. Once they are moved in and settled in, it's great when you never hear from them and they pay their rent on time every month. You drive by and the house always looks well cared for and they live there for more than 10 years. At this point, half your mortgage should be paid off and all the work that you had to do was the initial work of finding and purchasing this property as well as finding the appropriate tenant. I'm not sure of any other job where you work for a week and get paid for the rest of your life but this is why I love real estate! Make sure to work really hard on the initial deal, make sure the house is great for the people that live in there and they should never call you to complain about anything.

Long term rentals are usually 12 months or longer, are generally unfurnished and the tenants sign a lease. Most of the rights of the tenant are protected by laws and are of benefit to the tenant and not the landlord. The main point of a long term lease is that you get one family in there and they pay their monthly rent every month. It should be hassle free, generally. Financially, you will be getting the exact same amount every single month and can count on that.

Short Term Rentals (Vacation Rentals)

My new favorite way is with short term rentals, which gives you much more control over your property as well as a much higher income. You might as well manage the long term rental yourself unless you don't live in the same city as your rental property. With short term rentals, you are much better off having a company that specializes in short term accommodations manage that for you. Although it's a lot more work for the managing company, it should virtually be nothing for you to do. I really mean nothing but check your bank account once a month.

Let's go over some pros and cons between the two types of investments as well which is best suited to maximize your profits. These types of rentals can be as short as one day, are generally furnished and generate about double the income as a regular long term tenancy. The initial investment is usually a little bit higher as the landlord needs to furnish the suite, set up utilities in the landlord's name as well as more marketing and advertising.

The work is a little bit more involved as the landlord has to inspect the suite more often, after every guest leaves. They have to also be available to meet and greet the new guests, show them around, explain how everything works and be on call for any other questions. Although you can expect your income to be about double than that of a regular tenancy, the work involved is a lot more as well.

If the average two bedroom, two bathroom condo downtown rents for $2,000 per month unfurnished on a long term lease, you should expect about $3,000 to $4,000 on a short term rental over the year. Don't forget that not every month will be the same. You will have a higher rental rate and be at almost full capacity during the summer time. Summer season is generally from May until the end of August. During the summer season, you can charge double the rate. For example, you can charge $200 per night, which would equate to about $6,000 for the entire month. Slow season is the other months, excluding December, which is Christmas season where you can charge double again.

During the slow season, you would charge only about $100 per night and expect the suite to be half booked, or 15 days out of the whole month. Don't get too upset that it's not completely full. Use this time to do any renovations, maintenance work or take a holiday of your own somewhere. Make sure that you have saved the extra money from summer to get you through the slower season. Christmas season usually starts around the 15th, on the Friday in the middle of the month and ends after the first weekend of January. These are your double rates again.

With short term rentals, you can also make a little extra money in several other ways. You can charge the following:

- ✓ **Cleaning fee:** This is a one-time fee that will cover the cost of cleaning, laundry, etc. Usually charged at the end of a guests stay
- ✓ **Parking fee:** some companies include this as part of the nightly rental, others charge a nominal fee
- ✓ **Airport pick up/drop off:** offer the guests a service where you will pick them up, take them to the suite, help them with luggage, etc.
- ✓ **Half-day rates:** if guests wish to stay half a day instead of checking out in the morning, you could charge them a half day rate
- ✓ **Late check-in fees:** after a certain time, you can charge a late check-in fee or surcharge. This is for the guests that come in very late and someone needs to meet them late at night. (For the safety of our female check-in staff, we don't allow check-ins after midnight. You may want to consider similar policies)
- ✓ **Extra cleaning fees**: clearly, if a guest leave a huge mess, damages any items or leaves

the suite in an extremely dirty condition, you should be able to charge an extra cleaning fee

Be sure not to charge guests anything under a certain small amount. Charging a guest $10 for something would not be worth your time in credit card processing fees, emailing the guest to explain the charge and then further arguing with a guest about it. Guests find that to be cheap and nickel and diming and won't leave a good last impression. Decide what the minimum is for your company or your condo but make sure not to charge under a certain amount.

After a full year of renting your suite for short term rentals, you will see that the benefits outweigh any extra work. The income should be much more than a regular tenancy, your suite always in tip top condition and you have much more control over your own real estate investment by renting to guests instead of long term tenants.

Once guests check out, you will have to get the laundry done, clean the suite, restock any amenities that you have in there, fix any wear and tear for the next guests, count your inventory and so forth. The marketing and advertising is constant, you will need to keep a detailed calendar of the guest's reservations as well as the guest information and be on call to answer the phone.

Financially speaking, you make a lot more money as you can charge a daily rate as well as extras such as parking, cots, etc. Please check your state or provincial laws as you may also need to charge and submit taxes on the daily rate. In British Columbia, there is the HST tax that is charged on stays that are less than 30 nights. Make sure to keep detailed accounting of how much you have collected and submit that as often as you are able to. Don't let it accumulate for several months as it gets difficult, as well as heart wrenching, to send a check for thousands of dollars to the government. Although it is their money, it doesn't make it any easier.

Be sure to also check with all municipal bylaws to ensure that short term rentals are allowable in your area. Some cities have a minimum rental period in certain areas. You will also be required to check in with your strata or home owners association to see what their rules are on short term rentals, if they have any rules. Each building management company has different rules and different definitions on rentals, so be sure to check with each one. It's also a good idea to have your lawyer or attorney look over all of your documents to ensure that you are following all laws and bylaws.

I know this may sound like a lot of work and may not be worth it but if you leave your furnished rental with a company that specializes in furnished accommodations then it's a win/win situation for you. You will still receive a higher income but won't need to do any of the work. The company will do all of the work for you and you will receive a check or a deposit in your account once a month. This to me is the ideal situation!

With both short and long term rentals, you will also need to have some savings put away in case you need to make any major purchases or repairs. What I like to do is have contractors that have my information ahead of time and can send me the bill, as opposed to having the tenant call to say the washing machine broke, and then having to call around for a maintenance person and check out rates, call the tenants back to make an appointment, and so on. That is way too much work for me.

I have it set up where I have one company that does my maintenance work for all appliances and I leave the fridge magnet or sticker at the house in question. If anything breaks, the tenants are to call the company themselves and make arrangements directly with the contractors. They will show up, fix the appliance and then send me the bill. Please make sure that you know and understand their rates and that it's in writing somewhere, as you don't want any surprises when the bill comes. Expect each house to have one service call a year for something within. If it doesn't, then it's a bonus.

Do be prepared for those tenants that are the opposite of the dream tenant. You will experience the kind of tenants that believe the landlord is responsible for fixing and maintaining absolutely everything and will call weekly, if not daily. They will even call you when their light bulb burns out, thinking that the landlord is to come over and change the bulb. Tenants like that sure do take the glory out of having rentals and I believe that's why some landlords just sell their properties. At times it feels like it's not worth the trouble, but don't forget—it's a long term investment. Once you're retired and on that beach, you can then think back and you will be glad that you went through it all.

For all other plumbing, electrical, etc., I have someone else scheduled for that as well. The tenants are aware that if anything breaks down, they can call the maintenance person directly and schedule an appointment. This does save a lot of time spent on looking for someone to come and fix something, as well as keeping the tenant from blaming you for not calling the contractors fast enough. They have full control over when they call and will understand exactly when the maintenance people can come over.

There is nothing worse than being at home being a good landlord and getting a call from a tenant to say that the fridge has stopped working. Being the great landlord that you are, you immediately call around for different quotes to see who can best do the job. It takes a couple of hours for all of them to call you back, when you choose a really great appliance company to come and fix their fridge. You then call the tenants to see if tomorrow at 9am works for them. Of course, you're thinking of how great of a landlord you are, as you were on this task right away. However, 9am does not work for the tenant; could they be there at noon? You immediately call the appliance company back and they say they can do 2pm as they are already booked for the day. You call the tenant back. 2pm does not work for them either; can they come at the end of the day? You can the appliance company back. Do you see where I'm going with this? I will end up with a headache if I have to finish the story. Turns out the appliance company will be there the following morning at 9am, less than 48 hours after you received their initial phone call.

Although you are a great landlord because you took immediate action, the tenants now blame you because it's your fault that their fridge is not working. They want to be compensated for the two days that they were without a fridge and point out that it's their legal right to be compensated because they were without a fridge and their lease specifically includes a fridge which YOU have failed to provide. They also want to be compensated for all of their groceries because they were spoiled, as well as repayment of all of their receipts for eating out the last couple of days.

This is why I leave fridge magnets and stickers in the house and have them call directly. It saves me the trouble of being a booking agent for the tenants, and they prefer to be in control of these things as well. If you are unable to find a contractor that will accept payment after the work is done and send you an invoice, have the tenants pay for the service and immediately email you a copy of the bill. You must make sure to reimburse them for their receipts within 48 hours as you should be the one paying for this service to begin with. As long as their receipts are reimbursed right away, they will not have a problem with paying for a service first and being reimbursed after.

Another option is to be able to have the company call you directly to pay with a credit card over the phone. The main point is this—let the tenants be in control of booking their own services. This saves a lot of headaches and paying a bill is not that bad, as these things do break down every once in a while. This will also save the middle of the night phone calls regarding leaky toilets. Once they understand you don't know how these things work, they will not call you directly.

Your time is valuable and this investment should leave you with lots of free time, not wasting time making calls and booking services. I'd much rather just receive an email with a bill to pay than an email with a complaint that I have to take care of.

Don't get me wrong—real estate investment is not as easy as some people make it out to be. Yes, there are times when you get a dream tenant and you never hear from them, they pay their rent on time every month and will go ahead and fix all the little things themselves without bothering you. Yes, those are dream tenants and they do exist.

There are also those nightmare tenants as well. What I always remind myself with the nightmare tenants is that I would rather be me than be them. They are still renting while I am a home owner. They are the ones paying my mortgage, they are the ones giving me money and making me richer. I would rather be me than be them.

Even thinking back to those nightmare tenants and being where I am today, I would rather have gone through that temporary challenge that I got through which never lasted more than three months and be in a position to retire early and retire well. If I had to go through it all over again, I would for sure. Those people are still renting and I am that much closer to retirement.

You often hear about the rich landlords or the wealthy investors and you sit and look at them in their fancy clothes and fancy cars, talking about the latest holiday they went on. It reminds me of the friends I used to have, where all they saw was me getting out of my fancy car, in my fancy clothes, with my matching Gucci shoes and purse, etc. They all talked about how lucky I was and how I never had to worry about money, etc. Lucky? Did I win the lottery? That would be luck, but what I do is not luck—it's called hard work.

We heard another gentleman speak at one of my monthly conferences that I attend who finally understood how I felt. He owns quite a bit of real estate in the Alberta area and, of course, everyone seems him the same way. He also explained how most people don't see him or realized that he had to drive home at midnight because he was out servicing his own property. No one saw him get up very early in the morning to go and tend to another emergency at another building and work all morning. By the time he runs home to shower, change and meet his buddies at lunch at the fancy restaurant, he would have already put in five hours into his day as well as worked all evening the previous night. So while his buddies, probably along with my buddies, were out drinking all night and had only just woken up a few hours ago and headed over to the restaurant, we, the investors, have actually been working all evening and all morning. But no one sees that, no one is interested in hearing about that, all that they are interested in is hearing about how drunk everyone else was the night before.

Yes, prepare for a lot of work at the beginning and you will be lucky when you find that dream tenant at the beginning. That is the lucky part. Even if you do have a lot of work to do, it is worth it in the end. Get into a real estate group or meet other individuals that are also on the same path and help each other out. You will never get help from those friends that have no goals; they only see the successful part and expect you to pay for lunch because you are the rich one. The work you put in now is worth it in the end and I hope to see you on a beach somewhere where we can discuss and compare those nightmare tenants that helped pay for our pina coladas!

Summary of Real Estate Investing

- ✓ Value goes up without any work on the part of the owner
- ✓ Equity increases through mortgage pay down
- ✓ Cash flow from tenant rental payments
- ✓ Great monthly income for retirement once property is paid off
- ✓ Huge asset at retirement
- ✓ Full control over your investment
- ✓ Leveraging available through credit lines for emergency purchases
- ✓ Wonderful inheritance to leave for loved ones

CHAPTER 2

Basic Suite Set Up

Now that you have chosen to furnish your suite and have rented it out, let's work together to get it ready. The following list is what we have found that is the basics of what every suite needs along with the requests of guests that are the most popular requests. We will explain them as we go along.

When looking for a furnished condo to manage or if you are looking after your own, there are several things that are a must for each suite. This is from the point of view of what the guests require in each suite as well as having the suite set up in order to minimize calls from the guests regarding trouble shooting. The fewer phone calls from guests, the more time you will have for other things.

You may use the following checklist to ensure the suites have the following along with their respective explanations on why you will need these items:

Utilities

Heat, hot water, electricity: ensure that all utilities are hooked up and set up prior to the first guests' arrival. The basic ones like the heat, hot water, electricity are the obvious ones and you will not be able to rent the suite out at all without these things. Please do not be so desperate to ever rent anything out without these items.

Cable television is the next one on the list. A basic package will suffice and although we have never had anyone complain about the basic cable that we provide, be sure to get the package that you are most comfortable with purchasing. Most companies offer all utilities (cable/phone/internet) as one package so you may be able to get a great deal on additional channels.

Internet must be wireless. There are too many families or working couples that arrive on their vacations and these days, everyone is bringing their laptops. It does not makes sense to have cable as your internet because the guests will either complain and if they don't, they will absolutely be disappointed and just not say anything. A lot of people bring their ipads, ipods or other tablet devices, where you cannot plug in a cable. You want your suite to be advanced, not old school.

For passwords and usernames, the username should be the name of the company or some sort of marketing word that will distinguish your company. Many people, when they first log in to set up the network, look at a variety of different options. You might as well use this opportunity to promote your company and have the company name in there. For passwords, keep them consistent, such as using the phone number of the company, the phone number of the suite, or something like the suite or condo number twice. This way, if the guests ever call to get their password, this saves everyone time in finding it or losing it as it will always be the same number.

Phone: at least a basic, free local calling landline is necessary. Don't forget that a lot of people are traveling from other parts of the world and although they may have their cell phones with them, it is too expensive to turn on and use at their destination. You also need a way to get in touch with the guests and the guests need a way to get in touch with you. It is not necessary to provide a voicemail mailbox as what will end up happening is that one guest will be receiving messages for prior guests or they won't know how to access their mailbox, therefore the voicemail will fill up. It is an added job for housekeeping or the receptionist to have to go through each individual voicemail to make sure all messages are deleted before the next guests arrive. At the end of the day, the voice message feature ends up being more trouble than it's worth.

The best way to reach and send messages to the guests is through email, as long as the suite has wireless. There are also many long distance plans that are very affordable and if you can add this feature to your phone service, than I highly recommend you do so. If you do not have a long distance package, then you must have a long distance call block feature in order to make sure that the guests are not making long distance calls from the suite and you end up with the bill. If you do not have a long distance package on the phone, please be sure to explain to the guests where they can purchase a calling card and where the nearest store is. For people that are international, quickly explain how to dial out as dialling out from every country is different.

The above are the utilities that are advertised for the guests. Make sure to also include electricity, heat and hot water and other utilities that are basic needs of the suite. All those utilities must also have the company name on them so that anyone from the company can call for technical support and troubleshooting. You can't have the owner be away on holiday when a problem comes up with the utility bill and the owner is the only one that can call the company directly. This is very important: make sure anyone can access the account for technical support!

What can sometimes happen is an account that is set up on automatic bill payment, expires, or has been changed and the owner has forgotten to contact his utility company to advise them of this change. A couple of months later the utility is then cut off and it's difficult to reach an owner that is away to inform them of this. All guests will need to be changed to different suites and the owner will be out of that revenue that they otherwise could have received. Make sure that someone else has access to that account so they can call and troubleshoot and have anything taken care of so that utilities are never disrupted. Not only that but as an owner, I wouldn't want to be bothered while away on a holiday with a utility bill simply because there was a technical error in payment processing. That is what the management company is for, is to look after the affairs of the owner and their suite.

Cleaning Supplies

Vacuum: No matter what kind of flooring you may have, whether it is carpet, linoleum or hardwood, make sure to have an appropriate vacuum at the suite. Not only will the guests take better care of the suite but most people will leave the place somewhat cleaned up upon their checkout. Make sure that the vacuum is newer, mid-quality and in working condition. Every once in a while, make sure to check to make sure that any vacuum bags are emptied and not full.

> ➢ We had this one investor where we requested he purchase a new vacuum for his suite. His suite was mostly carpeted and housekeeping already has enough to carry, without having to bring a vacuum with them. Not only that but the guests needed something to vacuum with as well if they are there for a longer time. I even went as far as researching all the local stores to find a good quality vacuum that was on sale. I managed to find a great sale where the vacuums were $50 instead of their regular $100. I suggested they go and purchase that one. Of course they did but what they ended up doing was keeping the brand

new vacuum and giving us their old, used vacuum that was dirty and barely worked. I'm sorry but that is unacceptable. Don't be that cheap! You can't expect your guests to treat your property with respect if you can't treat your own property with respect.

Dishwasher tabs: A basic staple for a clean kitchen. As long as you provide two or three tabs underneath the kitchen sink for the dishwasher, then you can expect the guests to at least fill up the dishwasher and turn it on before they leave. You certainly can't expect a guest to go out and purchase a bag full of dishwasher tabs or dishwasher liquid when they are only there for a week or a few days. Buy these items in bulk and leave a couple for them to use. Although I said you can expect a guest to fill up a dishwasher, don't be surprised if they fill up the sink instead!

Cleaning cloths: Several should be left underneath the kitchen sink. If you don't leave anything for the guests to wipe counters or spills with, you can bet that they will use the towels. They need something they can use for basic cleaning around the suite as some guests appreciate being in a clean condo or home, even if they are on holiday. These can even be rags and don't have to be fancy looking, as long as there is something underneath the sink that they know they can use for cleaning.

Cleaner: A small bottle of basic all-purpose cleaner should be left under the sink next to the cloths. This doesn't need to be anything that the guests will call

PROFITS IN REAL ESTATE RENTALS

home to brag about, just as long as it's some type of disinfectant and cleans up basic messes. Again, the more opportunities that the guests have to clean the suite, the more likely they will do it and not assume that it's okay to leave a mess.

Broom/dust pan: Although you are already providing a vacuum in the suite, sometimes it's quicker and easier just to grab a broom and dustpan to quickly sweep. These are so inexpensive that there is no excuse not to have one. Yes, we have had guests that specifically asked for a broom and dust pan even though there was already a vacuum in the suite. Just provide one and keep it in the closet near the front door—that way it is always in the same spot, all of the time, in case the guests call to ask where it is.

Linens

Bedding: When purchasing and deciding on the quality of the linen, get the best ones that money can buy. If you have only one or two suites, you can easily afford to find linens that are on sale but that are of great quality. Don't forget that most of the time that the guests will be spending in the room will be in bed so if you spend any money, it should be here. I suggest purchasing white linens and having several sets on hand. We don't leave any extra linens inside the suite as the guests will end up using them and you will need to do laundry for two sets of linens and have no clean ones to simply change them with. Not only that but you have to be 100% sure that the linens are cleaned and sanitized and just because a bed looks like it was not used does not mean that it really wasn't used. We generally take out all linens and towels from every suite even if they appear that they have not been used. It's always better to be safe than sorry. White linen is also easier to replace in case an item or two is either damaged or missing as oppose to trying to find that one sheet or pillow case in a specific color that will end up not matching. You will end up purchasing an entire new sheet set if you can't find that one matching pillow case. Stick with white, it looks cleaner anyways.

Pillows: Each bed should come with four pillows. Provide two different kinds of pillows, as some people like the soft pillows and others like the hard pillows. This way, if there are two different kinds, then there is a better chance that they will have the exact pillow that they prefer to sleep on. Again, do not buy the cheapest possible as you will have complaints and will need to replace these ones more often anyways.

> ➢ We had another owner that owned this beautiful, three bedroom, large suite right downtown Vancouver, in the prestigious neighborhood of Coal Harbour. The place and view were absolutely stunning. Then you have the items that she put into this suite. The pillows were the absolute cheapest ones that you can purchase at Ikea; they were flat as pancakes and the inside of the pillow started bunching up in some spots, leaving the rest of the pillow with nothing but the material. We ended up putting all four of those pillows into one

pillow case just to make one pillow. It is so embarrassing when you have a million-dollar property and try to furnish it with the cheapest possible items. The entire place looked horrible and you cannot demand the type of rates that the suite could have demanded if it had luxury items in it.

Duvets: Please provide the best duvet that you can possibly afford. Again, do not be cheap in this apartment and provide a thin, tiny blanket just to say there is a duvet. Yes, Ikea does provide some nice, feather-filled duvets that we use in all of our suites. You should expect to spend at least $50 to $60 per duvet and these ones are not only big and fluffy but they do last a long time. A blanket is not enough. You may purchase another blanket and leave that inside the closet as a spare but do not try to pass it off as a duvet for a bed. Like I said, the cheaper you make your place look, the worse it will be treated.

Duvet cover/sheets: In our company, we use sheets as duvets and the art is in the folding. This was taught to me by one of the high-end hotels and it's the method that they use in order to save on laundry, decrease the amount of linens that a bed requires, and is cost-effective. They simply use two sheets instead of a sheet and duvet cover separately. They fold the duvet within the two sheets so that it appears that there is a duvet cover and sheet. It looks really neat once you get the hang of folding it. It does save on laundry costs and linens and if the guests are ever liable for replacing a duvet cover, their cost is only limited to the sheet, not the cover.

Towels: At the beginning when we only had a few condos, we purchased the best towels we could find. We also had two separate colors so that the bathrooms looked like store displays. As we grew bigger, purchasing individual towel sets was becoming quite expensive and the Laundromat didn't want to waste their time washing two loads of laundry for the same suite and having to separate the colors. In the end, it ends up better when all the towels are white, they are purchased in bulk so that they all match which again, makes it easier to replace and match color. Stay away from fancy patterns as those may be harder to match later on. Wherever you purchase the towels from, ask for some towel samples and try them out. Do not purchase the towels where when you get out of the shower, the towel does not soak up the water and all it does is spread the water around on your body. This is so annoying and frustrating and you don't want your whole company to look cheap because the towels can't even soak up the water. Try and test them out first, give them to others to test and pick the ones that most people like.

There should be at least one set of towels per person. This would include a bath sheet which is the large towel, a hand towel that would be medium in size as well as a face cloth or a smaller towel. Have each set folded separately and put together. Take care in folding the towels and ensure that they look like a display. Do not simply shove them in a linen closet but have them hung up as nicely as you can manage. Add another set somewhere close, normally underneath the sink. Always keep the spare set of towels in the same spot. You would be surprised how many people actually call you to ask where the second set of towels are located. If you have one set hung up on the towel rack, the second set could be on top of the toilet, on top of the counter or even on top of the bed. Pick one spot for the second set and always have them there so that the guests can find them easily.

We only provide enough towels for the number of guests that we have registered. I notice that during the summer when people are coming for holiday rentals, they see that we have two beds and the living room appears to be large enough for more people. In order to save money on the extra person charge, their method is to check in, ask for more towels and then ask for more linens because they are cold. Not sure how cold it can get in the middle of summer time but I have seen this excuse too many times. They hope that we will bring over all these extra linens and towels for their unregistered guests and save the extra person fee(s).

We clearly display in our ads that any extra linens or towels are subject to a fee so that they may as well register their other guests, pay the fee and receive all the extra towels, pillows and amenities. They will also say something like there is a stain on their linens and if we can bring over another set. When we arrive, they don't want to let us in through the door but want to take the linens and offer to change the beds themselves. We make sure to advise the guests that in order to bring over the non-stained linens, that we would need to take out the other ones. It's almost funny how many people end up saying "don't worry about it."

Mattress Covers: These can be purchased very cheaply and is one item that you don't need to worry about the looks or the price. Just buy something. It is cheaper to replace a mattress cover than an entire mattress or have a stained mattress. These can be cleaned every once in a while and don't need to be done along with the laundry every single time. That's what the fitted sheet is for.

In our company, we ask the owners to provide the pillows, duvet and mattress covers. We supply the rest, at a cost, in order to make sure that the quality is uniform in all our suites, all linens and towels are matching and that we can quickly go in and change all bedding and towels, without having to do laundry for the special towels and linens. If they insist on having their own linens and towels, advise them that there will be further cleaning costs to clean their specialty items. They will also have to provide a second full set of everything so that housekeeping doesn't have to do laundry in the suite, which is very time consuming. When we return the suites to the owners, the suites come cleaned and ready for their own guests and the linens and towels stay with them.

Mattress: Another friendly reminder that the guests will spend the most amount of time in bed while at your condo. Please make sure to provide the most comfortable bed and mattress that you can find or can afford. If the bed is uncomfortable for the guests, they will check out the next day, as some people won't be able to sleep there.

We had one guest that complained about the bed so much that we actually changed the entire mattress for them. Those same guests ended up purchasing an investment property and we ended up managing it for them since they were so impressed with our customer service. Don't forget that some guests may not even take the time to complain to you about it but you can be sure they will complain to their friends and families. Try to avoid this ahead of time and just provide the absolute best mattress you can find.

The next sections of the suite, we will go through room by room. These items will be things that you cannot avoid because if you leave them out, it will only be a matter of time before the guests call and ask for these items. Of course, you can skip some for now, but be prepared that the guests will eventually call you and ask you for these things.

Bedrooms

Each bedroom must have basic items in order for the guest to be comfortable. Yes, the obvious is the bed with the mattress and the mattress cover. It must come with the pillows and duvet, not a blanket, but a nice thick duvet as well as a sheet set. Decorative pillows are a nice touch and a nice added color to an all-white linen bed. If you can, add a small decorative throw or small blanket at the end of the bed for an extra blanket or just for decorative purposes. All linens should be stain free, always.

You should have at least one side table beside the bed, two is better. Guests always want a small lamp on the side table so don't skip this important item. They like to sit in bed to read, get caught up on their work or just surf the net from their bed. They do not want to have to get out of bed to turn off the lights and having a small light on is better than having the big light on in the room. Just think how this also saves you money by using less electricity! You can get a very nice decorative lamp at a discount store and don't need to spend a lot of money on side decorative lamps to make the entire room look nicer. The side table should also have an alarm clock.

A nice added touch is some art on the wall. Again, this does not have to be an area where you spend a lot of money. You can get inexpensive wall art at a discount store. Do not purchase wall art from Ikea as it's not always cheaper and everyone knows it's an Ikea item. It is worth the time to shop around but you must have something on the walls.

We did have a guest that although the suite looked exactly as it did in the photos, she demanded more wall art. You would think that guests would probably not notice this but this one guest could not live without any wall art in the living or dining room. Again, you would think that perhaps they sat there and thought, "Hmm, I just noticed that there is no wall art in the living room or dining room. That's weird." This one guest was so upset that she actually called us and demanded that someone come over immediately with wall art.

Inside the closet, you must have some hangers. People do come with clothes that need to be hung up and cannot be just sitting in their luggage folded. It also makes the closet look homey as oppose to bare, with nothing in it. It is up to you whether you want to add another blanket inside the closet on the shelf but you will have to remember to take it out after every single guest to make sure it's clean. Do not assume that because it appears to be folded up there just as you have left it, that it was unused. You must take it out, check it and replace it with a clean one. Assume the absolute worst and then you and your guests are protected. Do not leave any other items inside the closet other than the items that are meant to be there. It is not storage space or a place to put broken or items no longer in use. This looks not only horrible but it makes the entire condo look cheap. It's also a pet peeve of mine!

If the size of the room permits, add a dresser in the bedroom. We have often had guests ask for dressers although there was no room to put them in. If you can, even add a small dresser inside the closet so that the guests can unpack their items and have somewhere to put them. The shorter term guests don't mind but if you are there for a month or longer, you certainly don't want to leave everything in your luggage. Even something small inside the closet is better than nothing.

Any other decorative touches that you can add are a nice gesture. The above list for the bedroom is the basic and minimum that each room should have. Anything else that you add will be nice but make sure that any linen items will have to be washed and laundered, books may get read and pages bent and other items may be used and abused. The decorative items are just that, to decorate the room. Do not put anything of value in there as if it does get damaged, you may not be able to get reimbursed for the full amount. After the room is ready, have professional photos taken for marketing and advertising as well as to make sure that the room looks exactly like the picture every time.

Bathrooms

Each bathroom should have at least two full sets of towels. One set should be hung up on the towel rack, like a store display. Do not be so lazy and just throw them onto the towel rack. Take the time and care to make sure it looks very nice and inviting. Have the second set somewhere where they can easily be found such as on top of the toilet or toilet cover or if the counter is big enough, on top of the counter. Its best to have it underneath the sink but make sure it is nicely displayed even underneath the sink. One of my favorite things was folding the towels and making them look really nice. I actually miss that part of the job!

There should also be a **bath mat** and ensure that it's one that can be thrown into the laundry along with the rest of the towels and linens. Do not purchase those big fluffy ones because you have to wash them after every single guest. You may buy the nicest one but it should be white and matching the towels for a quick wash.

The **shower curtain** can be decorative but do not purchase the one that has the plastic holes for the rings. It should be a cloth so that the holes do not get wrecked and the whole curtain has to be replaced. You will also need a clear shower liner if you are purchasing a cloth one. If you do purchase the decorative plastic one, that is fine but do be prepared to purchase a new one every so often as those holes do not last a long time.

Toilet paper must be provided. Have a fresh roll on the toilet paper holder and replace it if it is less than 50% full. It looks really cheap when you still have toilet paper on a roll when it's almost out. If you want to be Susie Saver then take it home yourself, but leave a fresh roll for the guests. There should be at least a second roll underneath the sink and place it as close as possible to the toilet in case a guest has to reach for it while still on the toilet.

Also provide basic necessities such as **soap**. There should be soap on the sink and one for the shower as well. Some places provide the big bottles of either liquid soap or liquid shower gel, which is fine. My personal preference is to have the individual ones as they are safer and can't be contaminated the way the big bottles can be. This would be a personal preference and some provinces/states may even have bylaws with these specifics. The basic necessity is the soap but it's also a nice gesture to have shampoo, conditioner, lotion, shower caps, and other small amenities. These are all at your discretion. If you are using a regular bar of soap, this must be thrown out at the end of every guest stay and a brand new bar of soap provided at the beginning of a stay. I'm sure you could find suitable items at a dollar store as well.

Blow dryers are always asked about and a basic one should be placed underneath the sink. It is only a matter of time before a guest requests one so might as well have one now. They are a cheap item; and you can find them on sale for less than $20. It's also much easier for you to purchase one than to have a guest bring one of their own and add weight to their luggage.

Garbage cans should always be placed somewhere and it should have a garbage bag inside. If you don't have a garbage bag because you are trying to save a few pennies, it will end up costing you the same to have to clean that garbage bin out every time. Not only that but when it's in a garbage bag, it's much faster to grab the bag full of garbage than have to dump the garbage into another bag, and worst case scenario, you see something that you didn't really want to see! Some of our cleaners place a second bag inside the garbage bin, just underneath the other bag, so that they are leaving a second garbage bag for the guests, should they need one.

Wall art is a nice added touch; it makes the bathroom seem more cozy. These items can be purchased at a discount store so that they are unique and you know that not everyone has one. Keep in mind that the bathroom will have a lot of steam so purchase something that doesn't fog up so the steam will not ruin the wall art.

Don't forget the **plunger!** Do I really need to explain further?

Those are the basic and minimum items that you should have in the bathroom. Any other decorative items are a nice added touch, but don't overdo it either. Don't forget that the smaller the item the bigger the chance that it will also go missing. One or two items are sufficient. Have the professional photos taken for inventory purposes as well as to make sure the bathroom looks exactly the same in the photos as it does in real life.

Laundry

If your suite has a laundry room or laundry facilities within the suite, please make sure that this area is always clean. Make sure to clean underneath the machines, as far as you can reach as well as the sides. A lot of people seem to think this is a junk room or spare room but make sure it's clean and organized. Check to make sure there is no lint in the dryer. It actually surprises me how many housekeepers never check this and two didn't even know that dryers have lint traps. Never assume anything, just double check and remind.

We have had a few issues in regards to laundry detergent. Some guests are expecting the laundry detergent, and some guests who have used it will later blame it on the detergent when those clothes ended up bleached, shrunk, or ruined. You can purchase the individual packages at a local dollar store but then you also need to add a disclaimer that they have to use it at their own discretion and that you are not liable for what happens to their laundry. Then you have the guests who are "sensitive" and others who insist that you replace your product with a green product. Not sure why, but on the issue of laundry soap, you can't seem to win.

You will also require an iron and an ironing board, preferably a full-size one. Again, this is one of those items that the guests will eventually call and ask for, so you might as well have one in the suite at the very beginning.

Living Room

The living room must have the basics such as a ***couch, television, and coffee table***. We do suggest that you purchase a pull-out couch that is of good quality. The reason behind the pull-out couch is that you can market the suite for an extra two people, which is a big bonus for families that need the extra room. You can either charge a higher nightly rate upfront, or charge for an extra person and not need to get or bring in extra cots. What we like to do with this feature is advise the guests that if they have an extra two people, that they can just add one extra person to their reservation, but they will still get all the bedding and linens for the pull-out couch. It's a way for them to save some money on the extra person charge.

Although we are here to make money, we are also here to make sure that families and companies have accommodations that are more affordable than other hotels and find ways to package their stay in a way that saves them money. The pull-out couch is an excellent source of revenue for each suite.

If you have one couch, you will need to add either another **chair or a loveseat**. There needs to be at least two separate sitting spaces in the living room. Make sure they are comfy and do not put in your old couch because you want a brand new one for your home. The cheaper the couch, the more often you will be expected to replace it. Although not necessary, it's a nice touch to add decorative pillows on the couch, but be prepared to change them every once in a while or send those ones out to the cleaners.

Besides the couch, you will need an end table for a **side lamp** as well as a place to put the house phone. Again, purchase the side lamps at a discount store in order to save money, but you will still be able to pick up some unique lamps. Do not purchase lamps that require unique light bulbs. Not only are those light bulbs difficult to find and purchase, but they are usually more expensive than regular bulbs. If you can't purchase the bulbs in bulk, don't purchase a lamp that requires special bulbs as it will cost you more in the end.

Also on the side table, you will require a **phone**. Make sure to purchase a phone that is cordless and hopefully includes an extra handset. It's nice to have one phone in the living room and one in the bedroom. Don't forget that the cordless phone, although they do recharge on their own, will require the battery to be replaced every once in a while. They do get expensive as well; sometimes it's easier to purchase a new phone than those batteries. Test out the phones, both incoming and outgoing calls, to make sure that they're working before the first guest arrives. Also try making long distance calls to see if you are successful. If you are, call the telephone company back to ensure that there is a long distance call block so that you don't get an unexpected bill the following month.

Side tables don't necessarily have to be big and fancy. We use the cheap ones from Ikea because they can be easily replaced if damaged, and they still look modern and are easily decorated with decorative lamps. Make sure they don't look outdated as it makes the entire living room outdated. It's better to get the cheap $15 side table (as long as it looks modern) than something more expensive but outdated.

A nice *coffee table* can complete the look of the living room. Make sure that it does match the rest of the décor of the living room, but I don't suggest purchasing one from Ikea. Get something unique and this can be purchased from the same discount store as the lamps. A nice touch is a decorative item on top of the coffee table, but it's not necessary. We also like to include on the coffee table a suite manual which is an information booklet about the suite, the company, and local points of interest. We will discuss more on this in another chapter.

An area rug is a nice touch but a lot of work. This item seems to get dirtier faster than the average carpet and needs to be shampooed often. When you put a brand new area rug into the living room, whether there is a guest there or not, it causes a lot of dust inside the suite. It takes several months for a brand new rug to settle in but in the meantime you will find that it sheds and causes extra cleaning. I find that the suite may look a little bit nicer with them but sometimes it's more trouble than it's worth.

A modern **television** that can go up on a wall or on top of a fireplace should be purchased. Don't buy one that is too small as it cheapens the entire suite, but don't make the television the focal point either. Something mid-size is perfect. At this time a 3D television is not necessary, but the year that you read this book will determine the type of television to purchase. Basically, do not purchase the newest version of televisions but purchase one level down from that. DVD players are very inexpensive; you can purchase one for about $20 that will suffice. It's a nice added feature to the suite but certainly not necessary. At $20 though, what do you have to lose?

Wall art, don't forget the wall art. As I mentioned before, it was a big deal for one guest not to have any wall art in the living room. These don't have to be very expensive—purchase something unique and have those walls decorated. It really does bring the whole living room together. Any other decorative items that you may want to add would be a nice touch, but do not put in anything that is sentimental.

Don't forget that this is an investment property; strangers will stay here and your sentimental items are not going to be sentimental to anyone else. If they are removed or damaged, they will only be replaced with similar items of similar quality. If you put in a decorative artifact from Africa and it goes missing, don't expect it to be replaced with the exact same item. Assume it will go missing or it will get damaged and therefore, only put in what you are willing to lose.

Kitchen

Last but certainly not least, we have the kitchen. We can include the dining room here as well. The kitchen is the biggest difference between staying at a hotel and staying at a suite. It is very cost effective for families to stay somewhere with a kitchen as opposed to a hotel so they can save the money on eating out. It's also nice if you are staying somewhere for a longer period of time. In case you want to have someone stop by, there is a kitchen for last minute snacks or meal preparations.

Basic appliances are a must for furnished suites. A *coffee maker* and toaster are the basics and you can find good quality pieces when on sale for about $20 each. Try to keep the same brand and the same colors together as it looks tacky if every appliance is a different color. A kettle or an electric kettle should also be at the suite for the guests who don't drink coffee but who drink tea. As we provide both tea and coffee for the guests, clearly they require an electric kettle to boil the water. These are a must in every kitchen.

Optional small appliances are blenders, rice cookers, etc. Be prepared to thoroughly clean these items and to clean all of these appliances after every guest. Should these items stop working, you will be required to replace them, especially if you have them advertised as items in the suite.

When it comes to **dishes**, we suggest that you purchase basic white ones for the same reasons as why we purchase basic white towels. As long as they are white and round, they can easily be replaced. Do not have mismatched plates inside the kitchen as they make the suite look cheap, plus it's a personal pet peeve of mine. There should be at least one set per person, but it's much nicer to have two sets per person that the suite accommodates. The guests do not want to have to do dishes after every single meal. There is no need to spend a lot of money on dishes as these do get broken, so be prepared to replace these and have spares somewhere close.

Some of the dishes that you would want to have in the suite would be dinner plates, small plates, bowls, tea cups with saucers, coffee mugs, small drinking glasses, big drinking glasses, and wine glasses. Make sure they all match! I have stayed at five star hotels and the dishes didn't match which made me wonder what kind of a hotel I was staying in. I was thinking that perhaps business was not doing as well as it should.

Cutlery should be a set for at least 8 people. Again, the reason is because the guests are on holidays or are staying for work and do not have the time to clean after every meal. Also, you don't want the guests to load up and turn on a dishwasher after every meal because all 4 people used the dishes and had to turn it on after breakfast, lunch and dinner. The more dishes you provide, the less frequently the guests will need to turn on the dishwasher, therefore, saving the owner costs associated with power and water. Bigger suites should have even more dishes. At cleaning time, all cutlery should be put into the dishwasher, regardless of whether or not it "looks" clean or not. There is nothing worse than missing that one dirty spoon that someone accidently put back into the drawer.

Basic kitchen drawer items such as a **wine and bottle openers** are necessary. Spatulas, cutting boards, cooking utensils, full knife set, mixing bowls, oven mitts and other like items need to be in the suite. It will only be a matter of time before a guest calls to explain why they require these items. The more you have the better, but the above-mentioned items are a basic list of what should be included.

Underneath the kitchen sink, there should be a **waste basket** with a garbage bag as well as a spare.

The following itemized list of basics is provided here for you to simply print and bring with you to make sure all items are inside a suite. They are the basics that guests expect and will request. We usually keep the most often asked for items but we certainly don't need to provide items that only a chef would know. We strive to provide what most people require.

Checklist of Suite Inventory

✓ **Utilities**: cable, phone, internet, electricity, power, strata, property taxes, insurance. All utility bills MUST have the name of the management company as authorized persons to act on behalf of the bill holder.

✓ **Cleaning Supplies**: vacuum with extra vacuum bags specific to that vacuum, broom and dust pan, dishwasher tabs, dishwasher liquid, cleaning cloths, all-purpose cleaner.

✓ **Linens:** 4 pillows per bed, (2) fitted sheets, (2) flat sheets, duvet, duvet cover, (8) pillow cases, mattress cover, decorative pillows. Towels are two sets minimum per bedroom of the following: large towels or bath sheets, medium towels or hand towels, face cloths and a bath mat for each bathroom.

✓ **Bedroom:** bed frame, mattress, end tables, table lamps, alarm clock, hangers, wall art, iron, ironing board

✓ **Bathroom:** towels, hand soap, body wash, waste basket, plunger, wall art, shower curtain, blow dryers, toilet paper with a spare roll under the sink

✓ **Living Room:** couch, chair or additional small couch, coffee table, dvd player, remotes for television, television, side tables, table lamps, house phone, wall art, area rug (optional).

✓ **Kitchen:** coffee maker, hot water boiler, toaster, dinner plates, side plates, coffee mugs, tea cups with saucers, knife set, cutlery, drinking glasses, bowls, pots and pans, wine glasses, wine or bottle opener, spatulas, cutting boards, cooking utensils, full knife set, mixing bowls, oven mitts, waste basket with spare garbage bags.

CHAPTER 3

Paperwork!

Your suite is all set up, looking fabulous and all ready to go, congratulations! This is a big step and the rest should be easier. Let's get started on getting our paperwork in order, putting everything together and then we can let the world know that your suite is available.

Make sure that you don't skip the step of having the basic paperwork ready. This part protects you, the homeowner, from potential bad guests, protects you from your local laws and bylaws as well as ensuring that there is no miscommunication between any of the parties.

One of the main contracts that you will require, will be the contract between yourself and a managing company, if you are having a management company look after your investment. If you are managing other people's properties, you will require the same contract. The other contract that is very important is between you or the management company and the guests. This is important for both the guest as well as the furnished suite. Lastly, you will need to fill out and submit any paperwork to whatever company is looking after the strata property or the condo association.

Contract between the management company and homeowner.

A copy of the contract is provided at the end of this book as well as on our website to download. The contract between the management company as well as the home owner is an important one. If you are looking after your own property, you may skip this section and move on to the contract between the suite owner and the guest.

The main points of the contract that must be included are the following:

- Name of the homeowner, address and contact information
- Name of the managing company, address and contact information
- Date of the contract
- Clearly define the roles of tenant and landlord. The owner of the investment property is always the landlord and whoever is leasing or renting the property is the tenant.
- The address of the property being managed
- Inventory list, usually attached as a schedule, of what is included with the suite

- The term of the tenancy, how long is the company looking after your property for
- Definition of the rental agreement, in this case, the management company is sub-leasing the property to their clients
- Rental amount. Most management companies have a revenue sharing agreement, which is of a benefit to everyone. The more the company can rent the suite for, the more they make. If there is no rental income, the owner is not stuck with still paying a management fee when there was no income.
- Obligations of each party, who pays for what and who is responsible for what items. Examples are who pays the utilities, cable, Internet, etc. Who pays for wear and tear, who pays for damages, etc. Have two separate sections, one for the landlords obligations and one for the tenants obligations
- Costs, who is responsible for which costs. This section also states that the company can only reimburse the investor up to a maximum of the total revenue of the suite but not more than that.
- Over holding states that once the end of the term expires but the suite is still being rented, rent collected and the owner accepts the rent, then the suite continues to be managed by the company. At this point, to cancel the contract, proper notice will need to be given to the company. Check your local rental laws as to the proper notice

that must be given as its different in every region.

- All notices must be in writing and email is now an acceptable form of notice. Neither party can call up the other party to provide notice, it must be in writing.

- Termination, in order to cancel the contract between both parties, it needs to be clearly stated how a termination would work. The owner cannot call the company and demand their suite back.

- Rules such as whether pets are allowed, any other strata or homeowner's association rules, etc.

- Signatures and name written along with the date of signature

Upon having a signed agreement, the next step is to meet with the owners or the management company at the suite and go over the list of the basics that the suite needs as well as take inventory of everything that the suite has. Print the basic suite inventory list and bring along with you to go over to make sure that everything required in the suite is already there and accounted for.

Next, you will be required to write out an inventory list of every item that is in the suite. Use the previous checklist as a starting point and go from room to room, making sure that each room has a different name so that they are not confused. Make a short video of what the room likes like and make one video per room. For example, master bathroom, master bedroom, second bedroom, main bathroom, living room, etc. These videos along with the main inventory sheet for the suite should be sent into the office upon completion.

Finally, you will need to make notes of any damages that are already within the suite. Make sure to take a photo of the damage as every item listed on the damage report must be accompanied by a photo for future reference. One point about photos: take two photos of every item. One photo should be a close up of the damaged item and the second photo further away with clearly displays what the item is and where it is located.

Next will be the linens. Some notes in regards to the linens, if the owners already have them there. The beds need to be stripped of their sheets and the only items left on the beds should be the mattress, mattress cover, 4 pillows and a duvet. Nothing else should be on the beds, unless they are decorative pillows. Please make sure that the owners do not leave any towels in the suite or any personal possessions. Anything of sentimental value must be taken with them in case the item needs to be replaced, it will be replaced with something similar that can be purchased locally.

The owners will also need to fill out a sheet that has the basic information about their suite on there, such as parking, internet, etc. This sheet can be sent electronically and returned to the office or it can be signed at the same time of the inspection and inventory check.

We require at least three full sets of keys. Two sets are usually requested by the guests and one set is at the office at all times. We cannot work with two sets at any time; it has never worked in the past and will never work in the future. There must be three sets of keys or more.

While at the suite, make sure that the utilities are in working order. Check to make sure that the cable is working, internet works fine, telephone is in good order, go and see where the parking stall is, find out where the garbage room is and any other amenities that the building may have. Make good notes on anything else that the office would need to know or the guests would need to know when they arrived or during their stay. Forward all information to the office for reference.

We will also require a void check of where the owners would like their deposit. They could either leave a copy at the time of inspection or they could email the office a copy that we could keep on file.

The following is a checklist of what is required to finish up the contract to hand over to the reservation department or management company for booking:

- Basic Suite Inventory
- Owners inventory Schedule A
- Owner information sheet must be filled out
- All utilities are in good working order (check cable, phone, internet)
- Suite has been cleaned, linens and amenities set up

- Voided check forwarded to office
- Photographs have been taken
- Keys delivered and signed for

The following is a sheet that will be emailed to the owners to fill out but its best to always have a copy of this with you while doing the inspection with the owners in case they have any questions:

Owner Information

- Owner Name
- Owner address (if different from rental property)
- City
- Postal Code/Zip Code
- Phone Number
- Email

Rental Property Information

- Rental Property Address
- City
- Postal Code/Zip Code
- Rental Property Phone Number
- Parking Stall Number
- Buzzer Number For Access Press:
- Internet Provider
- Network Name
- Network Password
- Cable Provider
- Confirm that management company name has been added to accounts

- Phone Provider
- How many bedrooms and bathrooms
- Bed Sizes: Master Bdrm Second Bdrm Third Bdrm
- Square Footage
- Strata Property Management
- Contact Person

Contract between Guests and Home Owner or Company

Our next order of business is the contract between the management company or the home owner and the guests. This piece of paperwork protects all parties and guests feel much better with a signed contract for their reservation. This is also a legal document for both parties and their rights, in case any discrepancies come up. It's a good idea to also keep these in a file somewhere after your guests have checked out in case you need to prove who was there on a specific date.

The following sections are required as part of your contract:

- The guest name: This same name will need to match the name on the guest's photo identification. Be sure to include this rule in your policies.
- Address: Ask the guests to provide the same address as their credit card billing information. This is also a secondary piece of security, as their credit card will not work unless they provide the correct card.

- Contact phone number: it's a good idea to ask for a cellular number for this. It's pointless to have their home number because if they are already on holidays and you are trying to reach a guest, no one will answer your call if you are calling their house, obviously! Be sure to get a cellular phone number.

- Identification: Ask your guest for the identification number of the photo identification that they will be providing. This way they can go ahead and book with you over the phone or online, but will also be required to show the same ID when they check in. It's another form of protecting yourself from fraud.

- Credit card information: Be very careful how you store the guest's credit card information. Check with your local laws as this protects your guest. It is enough to provide the last four digits of their credit card for the contract, as some laws do not allow for storing the entire credit card information. Check local laws and proceed carefully with your guest's personal information.

- Name on credit card: Our policy is to have the reservation in the same name as the person with the credit card. At times, you will have someone's young adult child attempting to reserve a penthouse on their parent's credit card. At times, it's okay to assume the worst and protect yourself as well as your guest's credit cards. Have the same name on the reservation as the credit card and the photo ID.

- Rental address: You will need to specify the exact address of the property that is being rented to the guest.
- Arrival and departure date: The arrival date is usually the obvious date of when the guest will arrive at the suite. The checkout or departure date is the morning that they are leaving. At times it gets confusing when people use the terms "from" and "to". People always wonder if "to October 20th" meant that they are leaving on the 20th or spending the night on the 20th. To avoid confusion, use the term departure date.
- Reservation number: If you are using a reservation system, a reservation number will automatically be generated for you. At times, for accounting purposes, it's also easier to look up people's reservations with a number. This part is optional but helps out.
- Rate: Clearly describe what the rate is, all other taxes and fees and the total that the guest is expected to pay.
- Guest signature: The guest should sign on the same page as the credit card information, along with the guest name and address.
- Date: The date that the signature has been written on the form.
- Include underneath where they sign what they are signing. Is this a reservation or a reservation request? By signing the form, are the confirmed for their reservation?

- Include a copy of your policies and have them initial every page and include with the form or the contract.

Please refer to our section about policies regarding suggested policies or rules. Once you have those finalized, make sure to provide a copy of the policies to the guests along with the contract. The guests need to be made aware and read your rules and policies prior to making the reservation. Please always make sure that the guests are aware of absolutely everything and that you are not hiding anything from them. There is nothing worse than going to stay somewhere and rules have changed, without any prior notice. Not a good feeling.

Once all of the above has been done then congratulations! The suite is now ready for your guests. You have done a very good job and should make yourself available for the owners, and the owners should be available for the management company over the next four weeks in case they have any questions. All other inquiries can be forwarded to the reservations department.

Now let's get to work on the next property!

Chapter Summary

- ✓ Contract between a managing company and the investor (home owner)
- ✓ Contract for the guests
- ✓ Inventory sheet
- ✓ Information sheet about the property and the investor (home owner)

CHAPTER 4

Marketing a Rental Property

I have recently decided to pop my head into the marketing department to see what everyone does all day long. I do remember going to college and marketing was one of my courses. We studied things like brochures, newspaper and magazine ads, billboards, etc.

These days, things have sure changed. My head is still spinning from trying to keep up with all the new social media and other internet marketing tasks. There is Facebook, LinkedIn, pinning, spinning, tweeting and poking. I'm sorry but if this alone doesn't convince you to have a company manage all the marketing for you then you probably don't have a life. There is too much for one person to do all by themselves. The day I retire and don't have to tweet or facebook is the day I'll be without a mobile device!

I cannot wait for the day when Facebook is boring and gone. It has recently gone public which in my personal opinion, means that it has already reached its peak and the owners are now just cashing out, taking the money and will be leaving shortly. Good, I am really sick and tired of reading people's boring posts. Boring posts such as, "I woke up." Well that's great news: if you were in a coma! Otherwise, why do we care? How about, "I'm eating spaghetti," again unless you are eating a live bug and have photos to prove it, why do we care? It's also annoying hearing about people's kids all the time and the boring things they do: "Susie went to the park today," "Susie is having a nap," most people really don't care what Susie does, sorry. I think that I will trim down my personal Facebook page to an exclusive page only, meaning, the least amount of people that are on there, the better. Let's go over some of the most often used items in social media today.

Facebook is supposed to be great for updating people with sales or promotions or anything new that is at the company. If there could be any humor in that, it would be great. If people "like" your page, then make sure to offer them deals or other promotions. Do not mention anything about your kids or how cute they are, most of them are actually not that cute. Facebook is also another method other than a website to have a page full of your company information. Although most people have Facebook on their mobile device, they usually won't have access to your full website, or remember what that is. It is much easier just to look up the page through your own Facebook if you are looking for that information. Be sure to keep it current and post relevant info every once in a while. Do not bombard people with too many posts as people are interested in posts that they could benefit from.

Another marketing tool in Facebook is their marketplace or their ads. You can add your own ads in the marketplace section for free or make ads in the ads section. The ads section works the same way as **Google Adwords**. Have you noticed at all that when you post something like, "I'm engaged!" or changed your status from in a relationship to engaged, that all of a sudden all the ads on the right-hand side appear to be wedding related? You have cake decorators, wedding planners, photographers, etc. This is marketing at its' best.

You can make an ad like that as well. You will narrow down the region that you want to target, the age group, etc. so that your ad will also appear on the right-hand side when their posts are relevant to your ads. It's also a pay-per-click system where you are only paying for every time that someone clicked on your ad. Again, it's important to make sure that your website is fully functioning, user-friendly, and has the best conversion rate. You do not want to spend even $0.25 for someone to click on your ad, look at your first page, and then leave immediately. You will notice your budget is eaten up in no time at all with any new business. Take the first step to make sure your website is the best it can be before making the ads. You can also find coupons for first-time users in some business magazines, so be sure to take advantage of that first to learn how it all works. Do not be cheap and rip the coupon out of the magazine without buying the magazine. For $5 for the magazine, you can get a $50 to $100 coupon. Don't be cheap!

Another great advantage of having a Facebook page is that your guests or "fans" can post comments on there as well as reviews. This way, you could also interact with the guests and reply to their posts.

Facebook also has a marketplace, a separate partner called Oodle, that allows you to post anything you want. We also use this to post any vacant suites that we have and it works much the same way as Craigslist or Kijiji. With this service, you can only post from the area that you are in and won't be able to post if you are on vacation somewhere in another country. Best to have all of these posted before you leave the country as you won't be able to post from elsewhere. Besides, you shouldn't be working while on holiday anyways!

Twitter: next we have Twitter, a site to post quick and short messages. Much better than the full page of posts that we see in Facebook, these are short! Therefore, the posts have to be to the point. I have found that now with these short posts, people add too many posts. You will still need to learn about how to properly post messages, have short links to the relevant sites that you want people to go to as well as learn about the @ sign and the # sign and what it does. You will need to interact with others to have your posts and Twitter page known and remember to post relevant messages that people could actually use. Of course, don't forget to add this icon as well to your website, next to the other twenty icons that you will need. By the time this book hits the shelves, you will need a whole page on your website just dedicated to icons of various social media.

Linked In: Have you linked in yet? Here is another one. Repost all the same information but in this site. This site, I found, was to be more for professionals linking with other professionals. Now, I find that anyone wants to link with anyone even if they don't even know them. Not sure what this race is but everything seems to be about having the most "friends" or "likes" or "followers". LinkedIn was a great source for business contacts but now it's like all the other sites, be linked to as many different people as possible. With LinkedIn, you can set up your own personal profile as well as a business profile. Of course you now have to ask everyone you know to like you or be your friend or say something nice about you.

Now that you have spent an entire day setting up the exact same information on the previous sites, asking people to be your friend or to like you, now you can prepare another full day of doing the exact same thing with other sites. Although I am definitely not an expert on internet marketing, I would strongly suggest you just hire someone to do all of this for you. There is too much too learn in too little time to even tackle this. By the time you finish uploading photos, descriptions, and those meta tags or keywords along with SEO stuff, you will be out of the loop again because you didn't have "circles" in your Google Plus account.

Blogs: Where is your blog? Certainly you have a blog, everyone has a blog and is a blogger. You must have one also. You will need to set up a blog and add this icon to your page of icons, hopefully there is still some room to squeeze in another. Here is where you upload more of the same: description, photos, meta tags, keywords and so forth. This time, you have to actually write something and write content. Still not sure what the perfect amount of words would be as I am always hoping that I wrote enough but not too much and hopefully it's worth reading. Again, I put in deals that people can use as well as other useful information. Once your article (blog) is ready, don't forget to also post this to your Facebook, Twitter, LinkedIn . . . . don't forget to email all of your friends, family, and contacts to ask them to subscribe to your blog. I'm wondering if with all these times you are asking the same people to do this, if it would be easier and more profitable to just call them and ask them to donate a dollar.

So now that we have friends, followers and subscribers, we need more! Have the same people subscribed to your newsletter? It's a great way to keep people in the loop about current events within not only your company but the industry as well. Offer the recipients of your newsletter something that they could actually use. Do some research about the newest trends happening in your industry and don't use this as a general promotion of your company only. Give them news and information that is useful. They know where the newsletter came from and know what you offer so that if they are interested in your services, you will stand out as a professional in that industry. Just make sure the newsletter provides all of your contact information.

You may also post the same information to your blog, no need to come up with all new information for every avenue every time. Although you won't run out of social media to join, you may run out of content.

Speaking of linking, have you posted your website link to directories? Not sure who actually reads the directories but linking your website onto other websites increases your presence, which shows your website higher in the Google search engine. I have gone through my share of companies that have the almighty promise of getting your site on top of Google, but unless you are paying directly for the ads to be on top, be very careful of whom you hire to get your page to the top of Google. Unfortunately, I don't have any tips on how to find a good one. Even though some of their other clients are on top of Google that does not guarantee that you will be. I also found that the guarantees don't work either so I'm not sure what they are guaranteeing to begin with. With anyone you hire, make sure to read their lengthy contracts and make sure you understand every word that you read. The ones that you don't understand will end up being the ones that you would have needed to understand in the end. I did find that the companies that you hire for link building do the actual work and link your websites to others. Just make sure to get the database or list of where all of the links are and actually click on them to make sure they work.

I like Google for their Google analytics it provides. You need to add a code to your site and then it will analyze the work that you have done on it. Again, I would definitely suggest hiring someone for this otherwise you will be looking at all the data and not know what it means. I do like looking at it as it looks very official and looks like it does something. It will show you where a lot of people are browsing your site from, how long they are on it and how soon they leave. There is a lot of useful information on there so be sure to use it.

Google places is something else to add. When people are searching for businesses in Google, you will notice that some businesses come up at the top with information as well as a map. In order to set this up, you will add all of your business information and Google will first verify that you really do exist before allowing you to have Google places. I personally like this feature when I look for business as it tells me where they are located and a little bit of information about them. This doesn't need to be monitored as closely as the other accounts and you don't need to ask anyone to be your friend either.

Google plus is the newest social media. This one actually makes sense to me with their "circles." For example, you can have people in different categories so that certain posts will only go to certain people. Unlike Facebook, which I can't post what I really want half the time because I have my family in there as well as friends that I would never have my family meet mixed in with a few business associates. Although in Facebook I would like to sometimes post things such as "you suck ass" of course I can't because it's not very professional plus my old auntie will get offended that I used the "a" word. So I post nothing and just have to read about how Susie clapped her hands today. Good for her. I wish I could post what I really think of Susie laughing while she gets her diaper changed.

In Google plus, you can make these circles and even add your own categories. You can have a family category where your great aunt will be thrilled to know that Susie slept for an extra hour during nap time. You can post about those cupcakes that you baked and how you are volunteering at church, only to impress your in laws. Meanwhile, in your friends circle you can post photos of your girls' night out in that outfit that your mother would kill you if she saw you wearing it, although you are now an adult. For the business circle, you can post all about linking, subscribing, blogging, reviewing, etc. The whole concept makes much more sense than Facebook for sure. In my own non-professional marketing opinion, this should work better than Facebook and will be more popular than Facebook in the end.

With Google plus, you can also "like" certain pages that you see on the net. That is what those little numbers mean when you Google anything and it has a plus sign along with a number. It has something to do with how many people recommend the page. Have a professional look at your site and make sure it is optimized and user friendly so that people will add that page to their recommendations as well. There are so many different avenues that Google does, I am surprised that they are already not worth more than Facebook. I am just really sick of Facebook that I want any company to take over at this point.

Google Ad Words: Have you heard of Google ad words? This is a fantastic tool but you have to make sure that your website is user friendly! This is where the Google analytics would come in handy as well, to monitor what people are doing when on your site. What I like about Google ad words is that you are only paying for the ads when people actually click on them. This is where it's important to have a great site first. You don't want to pay for the ads only to have people leave after they have arrived on the first page. You can decide on how much to pay for every time someone clicks on your site (pay per click) and set a budget as well so that you are only spending what you can afford. You will notice that your traffic to your website increases very quickly but that your budget also runs out quickly as well. Get some feedback from a professional on how to best set this up as this is a great tool to use when you are ready to use it. You will also find coupons for trial offers in certain business magazines so be sure to use those first so that you can see how it worked before investing too much of your own money.

Craigslist & Kijiji: a lot of people post their vacant suites to these sites. These sites are great because they are local and they are free! Each city and region has their favorite way of advertising. I have noticed that in Vancouver, people usually post to Craigslist, in Edmonton most people use Kijiji and parts of the States prefer backpage.com Either one of these will work but ask around to see which one is the most popular.

Myself, I like Kijiji because I can store my ads there and repost them or move them back up to the top for a small fee. It's much easier than reposting all over again on Craigslist. In the "my Kijiji" section after you log in, it has all of your ads neatly displayed and shows on which page your ad currently stands. This way, it's much easier to figure out which ads need reposting and it takes about one minute to quickly repost them.

With Craigslist, you need to repost each ad manually. This part is very tedious and boring, however, for cities like Vancouver, it is what is used most often. The other thing you need to be careful of is to make sure that your ad is actually online. There would be times that I posted several ads and none of them were actually online. They email you a confirmation stating that it is online but in fact, it's not. If you post too many ads or post from a city that is not the same city that you are posting to, the ad will not show up. For this reason, I don't enjoy posting to Craigslist but we do get a lot of our guests from there.

Partnering up with other vacation rental agencies is another great way to increase your presence. One of our favorites is ownerdirect.com Not only are they popular but the ladies that work with them are all wonderful, helpful and genuinely care about the guests. Not once have we felt that they were doing something to increase their profit but are always there to help out and make sure that both the guests and the owners are happy. And of course, they are Canadian!

With Ownerdirect, the owner lists their property, adds photos, descriptions, rates, calendars and so forth. This company is like a booking agency between the owners and the guests, facilitates the booking process and once there is a booking, they email us the details. They are always fast with their response, are opened extended hours and any issues are resolved very quickly and in a way that everyone is happy.

Slightly South of the border is another booking agency that will not be getting an honorable mention. Although we do work with them they are extremely strict about their rules and have only their profit in mind. They collect the guest's entire reservation up front in order to book no matter how far ahead you are booking. They want all fees, deposits, absolutely every penny to go through their company. They don't even want us to ask our guests for a credit card so in case they destroy the condo, this company will only reimburse us for the amount of damage deposit that they charged the guest. This amount is usually to a maximum of about $1,000, which wouldn't help us out at all. Not only that, but of course they would take their fee from the damage deposit as they charge a fee on absolutely every dime that they charge. They are not easy to work with and quickly threaten to suspend our account if we don't abide by their every single rule. To top it off, they don't answer their phones but instead you need to leave them an email. When they do call back, they are rude and not even happy to help. I really wonder how some people stay in business when they aren't friendly in the hospitality industry.

There are so many booking agencies out there that you really have to go through some of them to see what works and what doesn't. Again, every region has their favorite and what works in one area may not work in another area. At the beginning, it may be a trial and error but once you see which ones work the best for your particular apartment, stick with those. Most of our reservations come from three of the most popular partners that work with us.

Another great way to increase sales is to find another owner or company with similar condos for rent. You may think at first that you are helping out the competition but they can be a good friend for both you and your company.

When you receive a reservation inquiry for dates that you already have booked, why not call your friendly competitor to see if they have the space? We charge a minimal fee to pass along a reservation, or see if we can rent their suite for one rate and charge our guests another rate and profit from the difference. For example, we will call them to see if we can get their suite for $2,000 for the month and in turn rent it to our guests for $2,200 for the month. This way, both companies are still making a profit and the guest has found a suite.

On the other hand, that same company will have guests that need a suite; they may be all booked up and will call you to see what you have available. This is another way for you to fill up any vacancies that you have— make your profit from renting your suite to another company and they will in turn rent it for whatever rate they could get. Having a great working relationship with another company is also perfect for emergencies in case you have important last minute requests, as they will be more likely to help you out. We have made a great profit year after year from just partnering up with other companies.

Finally, there is a whole other world of internet marketing. There are too many ways to do internet marketing to include here but I do suggest to do some research on it. You will need a website, then some search engine optimization (SEO), linking with other websites and pages, using tag words and many more things. Getting into this area of marketing will require some special help and is not usually something that can be done by the owner. You will really need a passion for internet marketing if you want to get into this on your own, I would suggest finding someone who can help you with that and discuss it with at least three different people, seeing what each one can offer you.

Chapter Summary

- ✓ Facebook
- ✓ Facebook Marketplace
- ✓ Twitter
- ✓ Linked In
- ✓ Blogs
- ✓ Google Plus
- ✓ Google Ad Words
- ✓ Craiglist, Kijiji, Backpage
- ✓ Partnering with vacation rentals
- ✓ Partnering with competitors

CHAPTER 5

Staff: Friends, Family and Real Employees

My favorite and best advice regarding staffing and hiring people is to not hire any friends or family, period!

Of course, you have a reason why you need to hire your brother or sister. We all have those reasons, just like we all have the same story after the fact of why we should have listened to that person that told us not to hire them in the first place. I am definitely not the expert on hiring people, especially since I hired all of my friends at some point and sadly no longer have those people as my friends. I didn't learn the first time, nor the second but sometime after probably the fifth time, I think that I finally got it. I hope so, because I will either be out of friends or out of money, neither of which I can afford to lose anymore.

In the stories that I am about to share, I will change their names. Not so much to protect the innocent as they are definitely not innocent but more so to not give them any more glory then they already think they deserve. These were my closest friends, the people I hung out with all the time, the same people that I talked to about my relationships, my finances, my hopes and dreams. I am very honest and quite often too honest at times. I probably lack the emotional intelligence that could be useful in business, the knowledge of when to bite my tongue and how to word things in a way to make people feel nice. I just call it how it is. Yes, I suppose it hurts people's feelings at times but in my opinion, no one needs to wonder what I really think about them. I usually tell people exactly what I think and expect to move on.

It amazed me how people's feelings get hurt so easily and then they don't want to come to work because I told them their cleaning sucks. Their cleaning does suck, how do I make that sound nice so that I do not hurt their feelings? I don't want to have a sit down and discuss ideas on how to improve or ask them what they think they can do to make the cleaning better? The guests say their cleaning sucks, so I tell them directly, it sucks. Let's find a solution so that it doesn't suck. Why is that so difficult?

I have hired friends who really had no previous experience in the particular job that they were being hired for but I thought, how difficult is it really to answer a phone or reply to an email? I'm sure that as long as I show them how it's done, then everything else should be self-explanatory. Just be nice in the emails, check your grammar and punctuation, and the email will be great.

We had my friend that we nicknamed Typhoon Mary. Every morning she was scheduled for 9 am. Now, I suppose it's my fault for assuming that everyone knows what 9 am means but clearly I had to explain exactly what I meant by 9 am. Typhoon Mary would show up anywhere between 9 am and 9:30 am, usually closer to 9:30 am and never at 9 am. She still thought that her hours counted as 9 am no matter what her actual check-in time was. I pulled her aside one day and explained to her that when we come in at 9 am, we are all here by 9 am and no later. At times, we have a couple of things to go over and we all have to wait until she arrives before we can go over everything. She confirmed that she understood and would be in by 9 am every day.

The next day she arrives by 9 am. I should also mention that every morning before 9 am, all staff usually arrives between 8:45 and 9 am. It's a very quiet morning, we come in, say hello, put on the coffee, hang up our coats, look at the day's schedule and get settled in. It's a nice and relaxing, peaceful morning. Until Typhoon Mary arrives, of course.

The front door goes flying open and hits the wall every time. Thank goodness for door stoppers as that wall would have a hole in it for sure! She rushes in like she is late, which in fact, she was always late, throws her purse on the couch, throws her jacket on the couch as well, her hair is a mess, she runs over to grab a mug to make coffee, spills the coffee on the counter, not all of the sugar makes it in the mug, milk is also spilled on the counter and then she puts her coffee on her desk. She advises that she will be right back, just has to go and park her car. I guess it's my fault again as I didn't clarify that being in at 9 am means being ready to start work at 9 am, not just being through the door at 9 am.

She comes back in and rushes over to her desk to tell everyone about her daily excuse of why she is late on that particular day. She should write a bathroom book, entitled, "101 stupid excuses for being late for work." After we hear her excuse du jour, we then get to hear about her evening the day before or about her drunken boyfriend, drunken mother, drunken sister or someone who stole their money, etc. It's now 10 am before we are officially able to begin work, even though she was there at 9 am and therefore it counts as starting work at 9 am.

It still amazes me how common sense is not so common. Once all of the other staff left the office to go and tend to their tasks, I had another one of those talks with her to explain what starting at 9 am actually means. I had to treat it like she was an alien from out of this world and the concept of starting work at 9 am means actual work is being completed at 9 am. This entire scenario is another example of why your friends should not work for you. It does not happen very often that other people would do that however, since it's a friend, then it must be okay. Since it's a friend, why be so particular about the exact time, a few minutes here and there shouldn't matter, should it?

For the next few days, I had to encounter the "attitude". She made it seem like I was the only one in the world who needed everything on time. She would come in at 8:30 am and make a big announcement that she had arrived, with the, "You happy now" look to go with it. She would grab her parking pass and leave again to go and park her vehicle. She would arrive back at 8:45 am and fix herself up, make a cup of coffee and actually be sitting at her desk at 9 am. Of course, none of this happened without the big, thick cloud in the air like I was asking for so much to have everyone ready to go at 9 am. I'm sure that doesn't happen at any other office, just mine.

I watched one day as she replied to an email and I actually timed her. It took her about a full hour to write this email. She was very concentrated on it, rewriting each sentence several times, using of the biggest words that she could think up. I had to point out that a lot of the words she used were in the wrong context but sure, they sounded close to the words we needed. Each email she wrote was a huge long reply and about half had nothing to do with the actual topic. I'm sure the guests would love to go sightseeing and see the Burrard Street Bridge and the zoo in Aldergrove as well as the Science World however they were here on a conference without children so I don't see how they would be interested. I also pointed out the fact that most people are emailing from other countries and their English is limited. I doubt that they would have an appreciation for any big words she made up and especially if they looked up that actual meaning and were really confused. I had to then teach her how to write a brief, business email. Again, my mistake as I thought most people would already know how.

We also had an incident where she was late meeting a guest. The guest and Typhoon Mary must have gotten to know each other quite well as the guest went on to tell me how she was a single mother and how she was late because she had to eat her chicken sandwich so that she wouldn't be hungry when she arrived and how her cat died. I don't know about you but when I travel and I finally arrive at my destination, I want it to be all about me. I don't want to start my accommodations off with hearing about other people's crap. I could not believe that this woman would not have the sense to only talk about the guests, their plans, their story, etc. Why would you tell someone your cat died? Or that you were eating a chicken sandwich and that is why they are late? Seriously? Even the guest found it so odd that she called me to tell me this. Once again, I pulled her aside and gave her my philosophy on the guests.

When guests travel and arrive, they probably have been travelling for several hours, at least. Some are local some arrive from a neighboring city, while others have been travelling for 24 hours before they have finally reached their destination. The guests are not interested in your marital status, your food intake for the day, or anything to do with you. We are interested in them. How was their trip? Where did they arrive from? Was their flight direct or did they have to come from other countries? Is this their first time in our city? What are their plans? Do they know anyone in the city? There are so many questions to ask them and get to know them that there shouldn't be a chance for them to us ask about us. When they do say, "Fine, how are you?" this is not a chance to tell them your cat just died! They do not nor should they hear about our problems. Most often, they took a vacation to get away from their problems.

While speaking with the guest upon their arrival, be sure that they have everything that they need. Enough blankets, pillows, towels, a working phone, they know how to turn the TV on, they have our phone number and know how to dial it, etc. Give them directions to the nearest food stores and restaurants. Make sure all of their questions are answered and none of which "How are you" means to tell them about your life story. Besides your name, they should not know anything else. This holiday or work trip is all about the guest and we should have enough information to ensure that their stay is fantastic! I will repeat myself in a different chapter on customer service as this is important.

Typhoon Mary also had no concept of time management. She was the only one who worked every day until 8 or 9 pm. I often wondered why she was the only one that worked 12 hour days and how she worked so hard. Either she was that dedicated to her job or her guests that she would put in the extra time, of course on my payroll or perhaps I should look into this further. As I go over the payroll every couple of weeks, I figured I had to do something about all of these extra hours as they were taking its toll.

When a guest would call up and mention that there was no soap, they need an extra pillow, and it appears that the broom and dust pan are missing, Typhoon Mary would take immediate action. She would jump up and say that she needs to tend to them. At first, you think how dedicated she is to her job and making sure these guests are happy. She would grab her stuff, grab the keys to the company vehicle and run out the door.

I noticed that she didn't actually grab the soap as the soap drawers didn't even move. I would send a text to ask about the soap later on when I realized that she was not coming back for it. We provide our guests with small, individually packaged hotel soaps but we do use a good quality kind.

Each bar of soap costs us $0.30, which is still quite high when you are purchasing them in huge boxes. Since she forgot to grab it, she thought she would go to a store to purchase them instead. This task of just purchasing the soap had cost the company an hour of time, $15 plus the soap at a cost of $3 as she purchased the big size. Her reasoning is that the bigger it is the longer it lasts. I enlightened her that these people are only with us for three days and they would never use up that entire big bar of soap. Once they leave, that soap has to be thrown out as other guests will not and should not use a previous guests' soap. Not only is that gross and disgusting but it's very unsanitary and in some regions, illegal! Therefore, that soap cost us $3 instead of $0.30 and had to be thrown out after their three day stay anyway. So far, we are out $18 for this task. She purchased the soap and went to deliver it, informing the guest that she would be back with the other items.

She then proceeds to drive around to look for a store that had pillows, located close to the condo. Again, although I am sitting at my desk looking right at the extra pillows that we have in our storage, it would be too much trouble for her to come back and get them as well as it would be faster to just grab them at a store. We can't keep the guests waiting too long. This is another one hour task, so add another $15 to payroll and another $25 for pillows. I do not like to use cheap pillows, especially since the only time that the guests are really using their condos is too sleep. We therefore strive to make sure that their sleeping is very comfortable. Delivering these pillows was another one hour and another $40 later. The total of this one task is now at $53 and two hours of our day. Yes, she delivered the pillows and announced she would be back with a broom.

It's quite odd that neither the soap store nor the pillow store carried brooms and dust pans. She was back out there looking for a store, close to the condo that carried dust pans and the broom. While I sat in the office, wondering why she just couldn't grab one of the office brooms and dust pans as we have extras, a pillow from our storage as well as a couple of soaps and deliver this in one trip. She again spends another full hour to track down this broom and dust pan for another $20 and go back to this condo for the third time.

This tiny task of soap, pillow and broom with dust pan took her three hours to accomplish and it costs the company almost $100. This happened daily, and she could not comprehend to put the tasks into one trip and grab the items that we already had and deliver them all at once. Her point of view was that she worked really hard running around getting all of these items for this guest. She had no concept that it was costly for the company and very time consuming for her. In reality, this task should have taken half hour at a cost of $7.50 as well as saved the $45 for purchasing items that we already had!

When speaking with her she was defensive like I was not appreciating the hard work that she put into this company. She worked so hard and there I was accusing her of not doing a good job. Try going out for drinks with your friend after that.

One concept that may be difficult to understand is the check out dates. When someone tells you that they are staying from the 3rd to the 7th, does that mean that they are checking out on the 7th or is the 7th their last night of the reservation and they are checking out on the 8th? There could be very many mistakes made when this is unclear. One of the very first things that we ask our guests is to clarify this as different people do mean different things. When sending out rates, we write that in an email as well, just to be clear. We would put that the rate is for checking in on the 3rd and checking out on the 7th for a total of 4 nights. This way, if they meant the other way, they would immediately let us know.

Not sure how many times I would have to explain myself but one of the last times was when this small mistake cost us about $7,000. She wasn't sure what they meant, made a reservation and we had a back to back reservation. Of course, the new guests arrived ready to check in while another guest was still in the suite. She explained how she thought they meant the other way and it's not her fault, it is the guests fault for not explaining themselves correctly. Mistakes like that are very costly. It's the guests fault for not explaining themselves correctly? Really, we blame the guest?

Our daily tasks are also on a big board. Not sure how confusing it is to write the correct reservation on the correct date. She figured that the 21st and 22nd were close enough and would often write a check-in on the wrong date. When the other staff come in and see one check-in on the 21st, do that check in and leave for the day, we then have someone else calling to say they have arrived. We are all looking around at each other wondering who this person is as the one check-in that we had, already checked in. After a bit of investigating, it turns out that she meant to write that check-in on the 21st, not the 22nd. So now we have a guest waiting and the suite might not even be clean for them.

These mistakes often cost the company a bit of money because tired guest who are expecting to check in to their suite on time as pre arranged and confirmed, now how to be inconvenienced and wait. Compensation can be anywhere from coffee gift cards at Starbucks to a free night's stay. Typhoon Mary now has to go and meet the guests which of course, now she is working overtime and can't get home to her family until late. Don't you find it strange how this only happens to her and no one else? She still does not see how her mistakes cost the company a lot of money.

After a few months of this and her large payroll invoices, I thought I would amuse myself and see how much she is really costing the company. Let's do a little bit of analysis and add up how much it costs to keep Typhoon Mary. After adding up all the extra hours it takes her to do her tasks, the money that she wastes in purchasing unnecessary items, the discounts and refunds we have to give the guests due to errors caused by her, the damage to the company car from all of the scratches and dents that she has caused, it turned out to be quite expensive. Not including her paychecks, but after we had already paid her, to work and hang out with my friend was costing me an extra $3,000 per month on an average. Hanging out after work was also not happening as much since we didn't see eye to eye on a lot of things, such as my lack of appreciation for her "efforts" and her "working hard."

I had to fire my friend, despite her big efforts and her hard work. She did not understand how I could fire a friend that had put so much dedication into my company. She was doing me a favor by helping me out, guests loved chatting with her for hours over the phone and yet I would fire her. I even had people call up and ask for "my partner." We were definitely not partners, definitely not. She still didn't see how she was costing the company that much money nor could I explain it to her.

The whole hiring my best friend to work together with obviously didn't work out. It cost the company unnecessary money to keep her and in the end we stopped hanging out for several months. Not only did I lose an employee but I also lost a friend. Not to mention a lot of money for keeping her for so many months. Lesson learned.

Well, until my other best friend, Sandy, needed a job and a place to stay!

Sandy was the Godmother of my child, we have known each other for about fifteen years. She worked really hard as a manager of a store but took the big leap of faith and quit her job, gave up her cozy apartment and moved out of the city to be with the man of her dreams! Sadly, she only lasted three weeks before she was back in town in tears.

She had no job, nowhere to live and no money. Of course I would help her, why wouldn't I? I definitely had a place to live: I'm in the accommodations and real estate industry, owned a company so I could give her a job, the whole nine yards. This would be only until she got back on her feet, found another job, etc.

I had her stay with me since all of our suites were booked up. I figured she also needed to be with a friend as she was very upset. It must be hard not having any money so I told her not to worry about food, as there were always groceries in the fridge and she can help herself to anything at all. If I went out to eat, I would take her with me, of course.

I figured it must also be hard just to live somewhere and not pay rent and to eat their groceries. She must also need some extra money as well so I offered her one of the cleaning jobs until she was back on her feet. I advised that I can't pay her more than anyone else and it doesn't pay as much as she was making before but its extra cash for her.

I remember her first day very well. Everyone arrives in the morning and we go over the days schedule and I assign tasks to everyone. I try to group condos together that are very close to each other. I wanted to make sure I was treating her like everyone else and not giving her special treatment because she was my friend. She was given the condos that were furthest away as that is where the new people start before you get seniority to get the closer suites. As soon as I gave her the two suites, she made the biggest face and said she is not going that far. "I'm not going to drive that far to clean the suites. If you want me to work, I will only do the ones that are closest to here."

Not only was I stunned but so was everyone else. I think everyone stared at me to see what I would say. Although I had no clue what to say, I came out with, "um sure, that's fine. Sandy, which ones would you like to do?"

She picked her favorites, grabbed her stuff and off she went to work. She was the first one back while everyone else still worked. I felt really horrible for the people that followed our seniority list and started off doing the suites that not everyone wanted to do. I felt bad all day but figured maybe I can get Sandy to come in at a different time to avoid the other staff. She did do an excellent job, I can't argue about that.

There were a couple of days at the end of the month where we had to stay in a hotel as the place we were in was rented and the new place wasn't quite ready yet. Coincidently, I had my fiancé coming to visit me from out of town, so I had to book a hotel room that would accommodate all of us. My fiancé was arguing the point of why I am paying so much to get a hotel room big enough to accommodate my friend. He reminded me of the time that my son and I were staying with her during the Winter Olympics, she kindly asked us to leave one evening because her boyfriend wanted to spend the night and be alone. So at 8pm that evening after working all day long, we had to move out of her place. Anyone wanting a hotel room during the Olympics knows quite well that you can't get one. We ended up staying in an empty basement suite with no heat that luckily had a futon. Now that it was my turn to reciprocate, I couldn't do that to her. My fiancé and I fought quite a bit about that but I was not the type to throw my friend out, I was a loyal friend, even after she had done that to me.

After days of arguing about it and finally finding a hotel room that would accommodate my fiancé, son, and my friend, with an area for staff and I to come in and work, Sandy announces that she will just go and stay with a friend. She didn't know that we were fighting over this in the first place but she did know that I did get a hotel room big enough for all of us. Now, not only did I spend all that money to accommodate her but now I feel like an ass. It certainly would have been nice if she could have decided that before I booked the room.

Other fun personal shenanigans that were adding to the pot was the time that she was moving out of town. She called to say she would be there on a Saturday and that we could visit right after they packed up the apartment. She called in the morning to say she was on her way and that she would update me about when we could visit. I had cleared my day for her to wait for her call and be on standby. It was her and her boyfriend and a friend helping them move as well as clean afterwards. I have to admit that my fiancé spoils me rotten and would never have me move my own furniture and would immediately hire someone to take care of that for me. I would also not want to clean as it's cheaper on our time to go relax somewhere while paying someone else to do the cleaning for us. Unfortunately for her, her boyfriend is cheap and would not ever spend that money to help her out. He would "help" her move her own stuff and "help" her clean the house.

It was mid afternoon when I called to see where they were. She said they were just finishing up and then had to do the cleaning. I thought I would be a nice friend and surprise her by sending my staff over to clean her apartment while the two of us went to lunch. I had my staff on standby waiting and told Sandy to call me when it was time to clean so that I can come over and help her. It was then several hours and my staff was getting cranky. They don't get paid per hour but rather per every job they do. They decided to go home and just wait for my call.

I finally called early evening to see what the hold-up was. She admits that her boyfriend didn't want to wait for her to visit with her friends and that they were already half way out of town. What an effin douche bag! Did it not occur to her to at least update me and let me know since she knew I was at home just waiting for her to call? Absolutely no respect for anyone's time. But you can't say anything to her about that as she would perceive that as being bitchy to her. Of course I hung up and was upset that my entire Saturday was ruined by sitting at home just waiting. I wondered how long I would have waited had I not called her.

The final straw was when we were at work and she was leaving to go and clean the second condo of the day. She was leaving around 11am and each condo takes about two hours to clean. She would arrive and start about 11:30am. She announces, "Oh by the way, I'll only be cleaning half the condo because I'm meeting a friend for lunch at 1pm, so you'll need to find someone else to finish it."

I have no idea what set me off but I just freaked! I cannot remember screaming at anyone so loud before in my life. I grabbed all my stuff from her and just threw her out. Screw her and her crappy lets work around her schedule attitude! What kind of a job is there where you dictate your hours? I have never heard of anyone at work saying that!

So there we go, another employee gone, another friend gone. I am down to about three friends now. Did I learn my lesson? Well, sort of. Don't hire friends. So I came up with a new way to find friends: befriend my tenants!

While looking for a tenant for one of my basement suites, I met this fantastic girl named Brittany. We were the same age, she worked as a server at a restaurant and we just hit it off. Not to put people into the rich/poor category but just to clarify some obvious differences. I owned the house that she was trying to rent a basement suite from, the house being worth about $650,000 at the time and the rent for the one bedroom was $600. I had a fantastic job owning this fantastic accommodations company while she was a server. Her little Volkswagon was held together with tape and I'm not sure if it even had a bumper. I parked my Maserati right behind her. I always thought that the rich and the poor could get along great, why would anyone take into consideration the difference in wages. All other things were just things.

Because she was now my very good friend, I thought I would be the best landlord ever and I renovated her suite for her. I ripped out a perfectly good kitchen and put in a brand new one. While her kitchen was being renovated, she moved some of her belongings up to the rest of the house and we would have breakfast together every morning and hang out. Although she worked in a restaurant, I would leave her something to eat in the microwave for when she got home from work. With her new kitchen, I added a nice fireplace to her living room and a couple of extra items, like a coffee table as she didn't have one. I would have a friend and tenant for life for sure!

One day I received a call from her, "Hi Evelina Mannarino, this is Brittany Cox calling. I wanted to discuss . . ." What the F? What ever happened to "Hey Ev!"?

I really can't remember the rest of the conversation but she was suing me. I don't think I cared about being sued so much as I cared about the fact that I lost another friend/tenant over something like $600. Only $600 and she would rather lose me as a friend and landlord because she thinks she found an opportunity to get $600 out of me. That was all I was worth to her. After everything I did for her, all the money I spent on making her place comfortable, she wanted the $600 cash instead. To this day, I cannot understand how people can sell their friends and that each friend has a certain price tag that they would be willing to take the cash instead of the friend. This would not even be the last time this happens to me either. She never did end up getting the $600 but I lost another friend. Lesson learned? Oh no, not yet.

So now that I have learned not to hire friends, not to become friends with the tenants, there should be nothing wrong with becoming friends with your staff. What's wrong with going out for drinks after work anyway? This happens all the time. I was going to be the best boss ever!

Shortly after my fiancé and I got married, we went to Italy for a month. I had recently hired an old tenant of mine to be the housekeeping manager. Wanting to be the best boss ever, I paid half her rent so that she could live right in downtown Vancouver and work from home so she didn't have to commute to work. This would help me out as well, as there was always someone nearby in case of anything. She saved travel time of going to work as well as transit costs. I gave her a company car, paid for the insurance, the gas, maintenance, everything. Although it's still a company car and meant for business use only, what do I care if she goes to get groceries every once in a while. She was given a salary for any incidentals or tasks that she had to do outside of regular cleaning, such as scheduling the other cleaners, tending to customer complaints regarding cleaning, etc. She was given the entire cleaning schedule and would choose her jobs that she wanted to do herself and distribute the rest of the jobs to everyone else. Anyone I talked to said this was an awesome job and I thought so too!

After getting back from Italy and seeing that my company hasn't burned down and everything seemed fine, I thought it would be a great idea to reward her. Since I was going to Las Vegas on a birthday present from my husband, I thought I might as well bring her along too. I sent her an email saying that she is required to be at the company's annual "business conference" in Las Vegas. Of course this was an all expense paid trip including the food at the conference. I thought we could dedicate one day to business while the rest of her time she can do whatever she wants. Boy am I ever a good boss!

So we met up in Vegas! How fun is that. I like to travel in style a comfort. I ordered us a nice, big Escalade SUV to take us to our hotel room. I like to have my doors opened for me, my luggage taken care of and travel in comfort and style. It looked like Jennifer was having a great time, especially since she had never been to Vegas before.

We arrived at our hotel which again, has to be at least a five star hotel. Jennifer is used to staying at cheap motels or whatever the best deal is at the time, more like the old Vegas, $25 per night type of rooms. I could never stay in anything like that, I would rather stay home. We have the bellhop take care of our luggage and bring it up to our room and the check-in went smoothly.

I had scheduled our conference poolside in a private cabana. We had our own television, bar, private pool, dedicated server and told her that I would cover all food for her during the day at our conference. Of course, this was immediately followed by our fancy breakfast over at the Bellagio, again, compliments of my company. After this trip, I would have a friend and employee for life!

We spent the entire day, poolside at our conference. We ate, sat in the pool, drank our fresh bottled water and discussed upcoming plans for the housekeeping department. I wanted their jobs to be fun, as easy as possible and with room for them to move up the corporate ladder. My theme seemed to be: "What can I do for you?" We laughed how maybe next year she could be driving a company Lexus instead of the company Matrix. We laughed and I thought, why not, anything is possible. In the late afternoon, we got ready to go to the spa for pedicures, courtesy of the company. We like to treat our staff like stars.

Although the rest of the trip was free time, I had one more surprise for her. I had booked another seminar that I called, "Exceeding Customer Expectations." Just like this trip, I wanted to exceed her expectations. I also wanted her to learn to do the same for our guests. Instead of the conference, I actually booked us tickets to the Cirque du Soleil show.

With a show like Cirque du Soleil, I wanted her to learn how the entire show is never based on one person. I wanted her to see how as soon as one person fails, the entire company looks bad. There are numerous people involved in this show that are behind the scenes; the accountants doing payroll, the marketing people promoting the show, the talent, the trainers, etc. Just like our company, we all depend on each other. I have included a report on that show in the customer service section.

After leaving the show, we came out the front entrance and Jennifer gasped at the huge, long line up of taxis. "How are we going to catch a cab with this long line?"

"Cab? What cab? A line? Hell no!" I replied. I walked up to the valet and ever so politely asked, "Excuse me Sir, where are the private driver services located?" The kind gentleman immediately whistled over a private driver and we were instantly in a private SUV already leaving."

"Like I would wait in a line!" I laughed.

"No, of course not. Miss Eva would never wait in line." She agreed.

I took her on a tour of the city as the drivers are a one hour minimum so I figure we might as well go for a quick tour. What a good boss I am, right?

We also spent a day shopping at Caesar's Palace, my favorite shopping place. After a while, I realized that we really didn't shop at the same places. If I was in Louis Vuitton, she was there just to look. She couldn't get anything at Gucci or anywhere else that I shopped. I certainly wasn't shopping at a dollar store either. I suggested that we split up to do our shopping and meet up at the hotel again later on. I was going out to meet up with a few friends and told her she was more than welcome to come along. We agreed to meet up later.

We got dressed up for the evening out, hopped in a limo and went to meet up with my friends over at another hotel. We had drinks, I had my usual water and we decided to go to dinner. My friends chose a new fancy place to go to. It sure did look fancy, and so did the menu.

I have no issues with expensive restaurants however I do expect the food to be great. I looked over at Jennifer who was very uncomfortable with the menu. "I'm not really that hungry," she announces. I thought I better at least order some appetizers so that I could share with her so she didn't feel left out. We ordered about three different plates and I figured she could fill up on that as well. Once the appetizers came, I passed her a plate so she can grab a few items. None of the appetizers were good for her, some were fish and she didn't eat seafood, the other food looked too weird. Okay, no problem I thought and ordered a big piece of filet mignon that I could split with her and claim that I can't eat it all so she wouldn't feel bad about taking it.

Once the steak came and I offered her half, she tells me that she doesn't eat meat. The best we could give her was a couple pieces of the asparagus. Although the entire dinner was somewhat awkward, I really didn't feel like paying for anymore breakfasts, lunches or dinners. I felt that I already did enough and this was free time. I also felt bad this afternoon when I ate my lunch in the room after I got back from shopping and she ate what I had left behind. I was starting to get a little uneasy about having to support this chick even though we weren't "working" anymore. So we left the restaurant and she didn't eat anything. Sorry, but at that place, I could barely afford to pay for my own dinner, never mind buying her a $100 dinner.

All in all, the trip was a success! We covered a lot of ground and made some new policies. I was hoping that this trip would also inspire the other staff to work really hard so that they can be the next one to go to the all expenses paid conference.

Within a week of returning and getting back to work, I received a call from Jennifer, "from all of the hard work that I do, I expect to get paid a lot more or at least get paid for every task that I do." I was in shock! Words cannot describe how I felt that day. Again, after everything that I just did for this girl and she wants more? Why did she not bring this up while we were at the conference? How much more could I possibly give her? I spend the entire week wondering where she got this idea from?

My theory is this: I started remembering how everywhere we went on the trip she would look over my shoulder at every single bill that came in. And I mean, every bill that came to the table, she had to look it over, although she wasn't paying. She looked closely at what everything cost, the SUV was $100 per trip, tipping the valet, bellhop, etc. She was standing next to me as I signed for the Cirque du Soleil tickets, another $300. She asked our server how much the cabana was, another $200. Breakfast at Bellagio, $50. My Jimmy Choo boots were $700. The list goes on . . .

My theory is that after she returned to Vancouver, she must have been bragging about it to some friends about her trip and my spending habits. Simple as this, someone told her that if I can spend that much money in one weekend and since I also told her that I could not live without her, why not ask for a little bit more for her salary? What's an extra couple of hundred dollars every month when I spend thousands on one weekend? I'm sure I wouldn't even notice this small difference. Go on Jennifer, ask for what you are worth and demand that raise!

My heart was broken and I was devastated. After all of this, after making sure she had a great job to begin with as well as perks such as all expenses paid trips, she had the balls to ask for more. Clearly, I opted for the option to pay her per task and immediately took the salary away and scheduled my own cleans. Each employee was very happy that they would get paid per task as I found out that Jennifer was getting paid the salary to do the tasks but had the staff do these things without her paying them at all. For example, if an extra set of keys needed to be delivered, Jennifer would get one of the other girls to do it for free, meanwhile, Jennifer was collecting the salary to do these things herself.

Looking back at her productivity, Jennifer had a lot of complaints about her cleans. When returning from Vegas, I booked myself and my son into one of my condos, just to go and inspect. She knew I would be staying there so I assumed she would make sure it was extra clean. I found the following items: broken frame under one of the beds, frozen blueberry in freezer, crumbs on top of the fridge door, a lot of crumbs all over the toaster, stained carpets, nice laundry basket with a bunch of crap in it like old computer keyboards, wires, etc. The closet had a bunch of mismatched hangers. There was a bunch of items left behind by other guests in the front closet.

While staying in that condo, as we arrived at almost midnight and had to leave by 6am, I told her that we wouldn't even be using the bathroom. They only thing she had to do was the change the sheets. When I received her invoice for her cleaning, she still charged me a full cleaning fee for the three bedroom and two bathroom condo. All I used was the bed and specifically didn't even use the toilet or towels so she wouldn't have to clean anything! It would have been nice for her to even say, "Don't worry about it, it's my way of saying thank you for the trip." Nope, nothing, she tried to charge me for a full clean as if I used all three bedrooms and both bathrooms, all the towels, left a mess and used up all the condiments.

Needless to say, the relationship worsened as time went on . . . she wasn't getting very many cleans and she wasn't making an extra money on the tasks either as the other girls gladly did them since they were finally getting paid. She blew up when I questioned her about company expenses she was submitting as well as the whereabouts of the company vehicle that was out one evening on a day where there was no cleans. She ended up quitting on the job stating that I was being unfair to her.

Her quitting was a blessing in disguise. The number of complaints regarding cleans have also come down. We were able to cut major expenses like paying for her condo in downtown Vancouver, less mileage and gas on the car and the salary that we no longer had to pay. Sometimes people quitting can actually be better for the company. However, another friend, tenant and employee are gone. Have I learned my lesson yet? I hope so, I'm out of friends!

For hiring staff, I have made some rules we cannot break. Absolutely do not hire friends. If you need their advice, ask for advice over coffee or lunch. It's not paid advice, it's just advice. Just like you give them advice when it comes to your line of work, you don't expect anything for it. It's as simple as that.

You cannot become friends with your tenants, landlords, or staff. There needs to be specific roles for each person. I now make it a general rule that I will not even go for coffee with my tenants or my staff. If I want to reward them, I can give them a gift certificate to a restaurant and they can go by themselves or with their friends. I might give them a coffee card so they can go and have their own coffee. I'd rather not join them for coffee either. So far, since I have implemented these new rules, I haven't had to fire any friends, lost any friends due to work, haven't lost any tenants, and I don't get upset if someone quits or gets fired. If they quit or get fired, it's simply a business decision which makes the entire company much better off.

Any hiring decisions, I now forward those to someone else in the company. I am no longer the bad guy when it comes time to turning people down. The company is not a charity, nor is it here for people to drop in for jobs and work at their convenience. If the employee is not helping the company in general, they are not fit to work for this company.

There are several people who are required to help out with short-term rentals, whether you are doing it as a small business or by yourself. At times, you are better off just to have another company do it for you because they have resources and access to a lot of items an individual would not. The following are examples of staff that are crucial to the success of short-term rentals, whether you do it yourself or have someone else do it for you:

- Maintenance: You will require ongoing maintenance of your suite. Whether a guest damages something or regular wear and tear on items that need to be fixed, you will need someone who can do these tasks in an efficient manner. You will experience clogged toilets, light fixtures that stop working, heating that doesn't work, towel racks that fall off, and numerous other problems. These will need to be fixed immediately. If you can do it yourself, that's great. Otherwise, you will need a maintenance person who can fix these things for less than a regular contractor.

As an individual who would only call a maintenance person every once in a while, your rates will probably be much higher as it's not worth it for maintenance to give you a discount for work every couple of months. If you're with a company, the company would have maintenance either on call or working full-or part-time. Either way, they would have enough work for that person where they would get the work done at a significant discount. Of course, working with a company, part of your commission will go towards their list of discounted trades people, so be sure to know whether it's worth it or not. I personally like the idea of not having to do anything and having someone else do all the work for me. It gives me peace of mind knowing all these things are taken care of and not having to receive phone calls about leaky toilets.

➢ While hiring a maintenance person, have everything made clear about what you are paying for. We had a guy that charged us a regular contractor's rate to go shopping for nails. He showed up at the condo at nine a.m. to hang pictures on a wall, left to go to a store to purchase five dollars' worth of nails, and screws, and went back to hang the pictures. All in all, it was over 240 dollars to hang a few pieces of wall art. After speaking with him, he started charging us 60 dollars per hour as of nine a.m., while he was shopping, and until he left. I wondered why he didn't bring the nails with him when he knew he was hanging pictures. Either way, he was kindly let go.

If you are the small-business owner and looking after other investments, it is your job to make sure that the contractor is charging a very low rate, about half of what the going contractor rate is for that job. He is also not to charge for shopping time, and they should be expected to come with tools and supplies already. Granted, some items will have to be purchased after inspecting an item, but for small things such as hanging wall art, they should already come prepared.

The contractor should also be available to do a job within 48 hours at the most. This should be discussed and explained prior to beginning work. Some guests only stay for three days and therefore will need things getting fixed right away. If the only toilet in the condo is not working, will a guest be willing to wait three days to get that fixed? I highly doubt it. Make sure that the maintenance person is available to come right away. The guests won't hold the maintenance person accountable; they will blame you if YOU don't fix their toilet now. And they would be right!

• Receptionist: The receptionist is the very first person a guest or potential guest speaks with. Whether you are doing this yourself or having a company look after your affairs, this person needs to be the voice behind the company. They have to have a clear and personable voice and must be pleasant to speak with. If it's a company looking after your condo, call in every once in a while as if you were a guest to see how they handle your inquiries. If you are answering your own calls, there is no need to have a separate phone either. You can subscribe to a company that has an automated message, where they press a certain button to reach you. Your personal phone will still ring; however, when you answer it, it will let you know it's a business call and you can decide whether you want to take the call or not. Please do not answer the call if you are in a busy restaurant, which is so unprofessional! Let it go to voicemail and call back when you are in a quiet area without any interruptions. There is nothing more annoying than having to listen to background noise while you are trying to explain yourself when you could have left a message and then could quickly be called back. Answering a call in a restaurant just makes you sound desperate. It's more professional to let them leave a message and to promptly call back. This service should not cost you more than 50 dollars per month. They do have live receptionists but I don't find them worth the money.

Calling back promptly means no more than two hours. It really shouldn't be more than an hour, but two at the most. You need to imagine the guest calling, such as when you are a guest calling around. You have a couple of companies picked out and you start calling them. The first one answers in a restaurant with a lot of background noise. You think, 'Wow, not sure if I want to stay there.' The second person answers right away and promises to email you some information. The third person you left a message for and they returned your call within the hour. The fourth person you left a message for called you late in the evening, about seven p.m. your time. Just from the calls, I would want to go with either option two or three. The person who called really late waited all day to call back, which makes you wonder how long it would take them to call back if your toilet was overflowing or you ran into other issues. The timing of answering calls and returning calls is very crucial.

Make sure either you or the secretary knows how to write a professional email. There should be no slang and definitely no spelling mistakes. In this day and age of spell check, there should not be one spelling mistake, ever. All emails should be clear with a lot of information so there are not too many emails going back and forth and wasting time. There is nothing more annoying when I email for availability and then they email back to say, yes, it's available. The next obvious question is how much? Make sure there is enough information within the first email for them to be able to book without them having to read a huge email before they even booked. The quality of the email should reflect the quality of the company.

These days most major companies hire their phone staff from overseas. Not sure how I came across this, but it's the best thing I have ever discovered. You can hire a full-time employee from overseas for about nine dollars per hour if hiring through a company. This company would be responsible for their staff. However, it doesn't keep the employee from not showing up for work or coming in late. Although they claim they can replace an employee if one becomes ill or doesn't come in, how is that person going to show up at nine a.m. and know what to do? You are pretty much screwed for the day if they do not come in.

> Some of those companies will also still expect you to pay for the day they don't show up for work as its part of their monthly package. So, not only does that person not show up, you still have to pay them for that day as well as work that day yourself. They have makeup days where they would send you another staff member if the original staff missed more than three days. After missing those three days and sending you a staff member to "make up" those days, you still have to show up for work and train that temporary worker and work the entire day yourself. They also don't work on the weekends. This company provided me with an employee that would show up four out of the five days every single week. They would screw up my whole day because as I was heading out the door, I would be notified that my staff is not coming in, which means,

I am not only paying someone to work that day, I am going to be working that day myself. So I head back in, get settled into my office again, and begin cancelling appointments for the day.

I do prefer the companies you pay to find you an employee, and that employee answers to you directly. You pay the one-time fee for them to find the employee for you, and then you pay the employee directly. This gives you control over how to structure their contract, and their hourly rate now goes down to anywhere from three dollars and up. At this rate, you don't have an excuse not to hire someone. The only disclaimer is that they will replace the employee within 30 days if you are not happy with them or the employee doesn't like their job. Unfortunately, most people like to quit within 60 to 90 days, and then you have lost that placement fee and need to start over again.

I am definitely not an expert on hiring and retaining staff. I am still learning that part myself. I find that a lot of people take the job to try it out and then don't like it after two or three months and quit on the spot. You would not believe how many times I have heard a staff member tell me that their long-lost mother or father has recently found them and are taking them on an immediate surprise trip to catch up and bond. Seriously, after the third time I heard the same story from a third employee, I figured something was up. If you hear this story yourself, chances are it might not be true. I don't think I ever had a job where I came in and announced that someone was taking me on a surprise trip and I am leaving immediately, back in two weeks. Where is that even acceptable? How do you even book a trip for someone who works full-time and expect them to just get the time off without any warning? Or that even perhaps they need the money and can't just get up and go? Weird people . . .

When you have staff that work for you online, it is extremely important to assume they will quit on the spot and take everything with them. They will need their own unique logins so they can't access a main system, and you still have the main passwords for all things you use. Your files need to be backed up frequently, and you still need full control over everything. Have one email address that is unique to you and you only in case the staff changed passwords on you before they quit and you can't access certain sites. Eventually, an email will have to be sent to your personal email box for verification in order for you to access those sites again.

While working on their employment contracts, include a clause that states they don't get paid if they quit on the spot. That money will be used towards hiring a new permanent staff or a temporary employee as well as training of a new person and taking the time to change and update all passwords from the old to the new employee. Make sure that pay days are several days after a pay period so that you don't pay them for the last day they worked and then they quit. They need to have at least several days of work banked so if they quit, they will have something to lose as well.

- Cleaning staff: Our biggest complaints we ever received were to do with cleaning. I do have a little confession to make that when I first started I did all my own cleaning. How hard can it be, and besides, I was a perfectionist. I was a little disappointed and surprised at how many complaints I received regarding my own cleaning. I had to transfer myself to another department as cleaning was not my specialty.

Even when I hired other cleaners, I didn't think it was important to explain how to clean as a professional cleaner should know how to clean better than myself. What am I going to tell them anyway? When it comes to cleaning and how things are to be done, you must write a manual entitled, Cleaning For Dummies. Some people clearly have never stayed in a five-star hotel, or even a four-star for that matter.

I had some beds made that looked like a teenager's room where the pillows are flat on the bed and the duvet is spread flat across the bed from top to bottom. It wasn't even smoothed out, just thrown on there. Never mind how the sheets looked. The towels weren't even folded nice and were put away into the linen closet as opposed to hanging on the racks. One day to my horror, I noticed that they took a top sheet of a used bed and used it as a sheet on another bed while the other bed didn't even have a fitted sheet. I thought they were kidding, but they were serious. They said the dryer didn't work. Well, of course, it won't if you never clean the lint trap. And these are professional cleaners? They were fired on the spot.

I then had to teach and explain to new staff how to make the beds. The beds should look like a linen store display: nice, big, fluffy pillows sitting up on the bed, at least four per bed. The fitted sheet as a fitted sheet and the top sheet and duvet folded over and down about three-fourths of the way from the top. If you don't know what I mean, go to a linen store and take a photo of the display bed and include that in the manual so they can visually see how the bed is supposed to look. Please refer to our policies section and look for a copy of our manual in there. Feel free to adjust the manual however you need it to fit into your specific condo suite.

It is important to stress how every suite must be immaculate for the guests. Guests will always find that one item that was not cleaned or was missed, and they will complain about it. I always told the cleaners that their job is of great importance. A clean suite is a basic luxury every guest is entitled to. No one will ever call in and compliment how clean the suite was, but if you leave even one tiny hair behind, you bet they will call and complain. It's a thankless job but an extremely important one.

- Marketing: Now that everything is set up and everyone is ready to go, you certainly need someone who can help you with marketing. After all, if no one knows you exist, how can anyone call you and book your suite?

Throughout my hiring and firing processes, I have learned that many marketing people are not capable of doing all Internet-related tasks. They can either update your website or post on your Facebook, but they can't seem to do both. Part of that is my own ignorance in understanding the differences between web developers, web designers, Internet marketers, SEO specialists, social media gurus, and so forth. There are so many jobs, but generally, one person can't do it all.

When starting out, you will require at least a website for people to see your photos and a description of your suite. If you have more than one furnished rental, you will also require a reservation system. You don't necessarily need to find a website developer to make a website for you. There are currently numerous other websites that already have templates of websites. All you need to do is upload the photos, the description, leave your contact info, and your website is done. Some of these are even free!

All you need to do is choose a domain name, have it registered, and you have a website. If you can afford it, hire someone to make sure it's optimized for search engines and that it's user-friendly. Have your friends or family try it out and give you feedback. Don't hire them!

Finally, with all of the millions you will now have, be sure to speak with a bookkeeper, but hopefully an accountant ahead of time. You will need some advice on how to set up your books and accounts and how to best run your company, financially speaking.

Be sure to interview several accountants. My mistake was to trust the very first accountant I hired who assured me they would help me out. Most of these are just bookkeepers who just keep track of what you send them. They don't actually look at what you're spending or how you're spending it, but just file whatever you hand them. Heck, I already had a Matrix but still bought a Maserati and an Escalade. No accountant advised me against spending that kind of money, which I wasn't even making to begin with! Get some opinions from other customers who actually use them to see what they say. I hired another bookkeeper from a tip from a friend who ended up not really knowing what she was doing. Turns out that my friend hadn't actually used her, they just attended the same church.

Do your homework on accountants and make sure they will advise you of what you make, how to spend the money, and set up your accounts so that you are minimizing your tax bill.

Chapter Summary

- ✓ Handyman
- ✓ Receptionist
- ✓ Cleaning staff
- ✓ Marketing, Internet
- ✓ Bookkeeper

CHAPTER 6
Customer Service

I find there are simply not enough books written specifically on customer service, with real-life examples. I have read plenty of books on companies and their "culture" and "customer experience", but there is not enough with ones that give you a real-life example.

Sure, we can all put fresh flowers in the room for the guests, which is a nice gesture. But what about if they call you screaming that they are allergic and they expect to be compensated for the experience of having an allergic reaction? What about if we gift a bottle of wine to an alcoholic? There are so many nice gestures that we personally may think are nice but may not be so nice to the guests.

Guests come to visit and stay with us for numerous reasons. They are on a long holiday with their families; they are relocating to a new city; they are here on temporary work but had to leave their families back home; their homes flooded and they require temporary accommodations. Maybe they got kicked out of the house and need a temporary home. Although the reasons are numerous, at the end of the day the guests' expectations are generally the same.

The most basic and expected, as well as unappreciated expectation, is a clean room. This is the very minimum a guest should be receiving. Although a lot of work goes into providing a clean suite, one mistake and the guest will not forgive you. The suites must be immaculate, right down to the bottom kitchen drawer, back corner, where they will find that crumb. And trust me, they will find it.

This is not an area where good enough is good enough. You must hire the absolute best cleaners and must have standards to be followed. If you are a cleaner yourself and you have received more than three complaints, please fire yourself. This happened to me, and I owned the company. This department is not a matter of someone's opinion; it is a matter of what the guests are saying. If they say the suite is dirty, then the suite is dirty.

There were many times I ended up arguing with a cleaner because they claimed the suite was clean and the guest claimed it was dirty. Does it matter in this case who is right? The point is, the guest is the one paying us, not the other way around. If the guest says it's dirty then it is deemed dirty. We strive to make sure we do not get any complaints to begin with, but it does happen that a cleaner could have missed something.

It has happened to me as well in major hotels where a cleaner would have missed a couple of things. The hotel room that wasn't very well-cleaned, I still remember not enjoying having to start out my trip with a dirty hotel room, and things seemed to go downhill from there. There isn't too much you can do to compensate, as either way, the guests do remember the dirty parts of the suites.

I understand that we are not all perfect but guests should not have to experience missed corners while staying with you. This department is extremely important and you do not want the guests to start out their stay with you in this way. Like I said, you can compensate the guest all you want, but they will never forget and only sometimes forgive you for the dirty suite. One hotel that I checked into was dirty and although I was compensated with chocolate strawberries and a free upgrade, I still remember the dirty room and I would have rather paid the full amount and had a clean room. Most of our guests feel the same way.

To ensure a clean room, we have a checklist that all cleaners must follow. Do not assume that because someone is a cleaner, they will know how to clean. Every detail must be written down and it must be in a step by step format. Although we do have this checklist, the cleaners will still "forget" to bring it with them or will still miss some steps. They end up getting so comfortable in their cleaning that they feel that they don't need to refer to their checklist and will at times forget or miss something. I have included the checklist in chapter 10 under contracts and manuals. Please feel free to use this checklist for your own suites or properties and make amendments as necessary.

We have each room checked over twice. The first time is when they clean according to the checklist and the second time prior to the guests checking in. We have a guest representative go to the suite a few minutes earlier to go over everything that the last cleaner did in case there was anything missed. By the time we have a guest call or email us to advise that a suite is dirty, this to us means that two people have now not done their job according to policy and this is a very big deal. We do not take these complaints lightly at all because the cleaner ends up not getting paid for their clean and the guests get a part of their cleaning fees refunded. The suite also has to be tended to for the third time, by now a third person, to ensure the job gets done correctly. What we don't do is play the game of "who done it" with the staff or the cleaners. They are to figure it out amongst themselves and figure out who will get paid for what. As this is a major pain in the butt for the staff as well, they make sure that the suite gets cleaned the first time according to policy. The staff will also look out for each other by looking over the suite prior to check in as it's also time consuming for them to have to re-clean someone's original job and figure out who will get paid for what.

Although the staff watches out for each other, you are still required to have another third party check up on them as well, just to confirm everything. After a guest is checked in, we still have a guest service representative call the guests to see how everything went. We want to make sure that their entire check-in procedure went well and that they are happy with their suite. Don't forget, this is their home away from home and quite often they don't know anyone when they arrive in the city. It's always a nice gesture to call them and let them know that we are here to help them with anything that they may require. This way, they feel like they have a friend in the city and can call us up for any reason. Being a home away from home, we strive to minimize the lonely feeling in the big city.

Please make sure to go to the next chapter and go through the detailed cleaning policy that we have and feel free to make changes or edits that will suit your particular needs. If you do the cleaning yourself, try to have someone else call the guests to see how everything went. I strongly suggest that you do not call them yourself in case they tell you that the cleaning sucks and you get defensive right away, knowing that you were the one that cleaned it. The absolute last thing you want to do is make excuses for anything that they tell you. The guests are actually telling you this to help you or your business and are in no way blaming you for anything. Listen to what they have to say, make notes and find ways to improve this. It is a blessing to have a guest take the time out of their schedule to provide these notes and suggestions for you so that you can tend to these items and the stay for the next guest will be that much better. Listen to them and find ways to help them and do not find excuses to offer them. They want to know that you are actively listening and truly care about what they have to say.

There is nothing more frustrating than when I take the time to make notes on how a particular hotel could improve their services and their level of cleaning and the manager looked like he couldn't care less how the hotel did. Sure, we received chocolate covered strawberries, fantastic, but what I really wanted was a clean room and a good 'ol, "thanks so much for taking the time to let us know these things." This particular hotel not only wasn't very clean but the overall hotel service by all staff was the same, they couldn't care less. Each guest wants to be treated like they matter, no matter what level of service they pay for. These things are quite easy to do, especially since listening is the most important thing and the one that takes the least amount of effort. Or so you would think . . .

Check-In Procedure

Imagine yourself flying with your family to a country that you have never been to before. You have already paid for your accommodations in full and enjoyed speaking with and emailing your guest representative back and forth. You finally arrive in the city and are at the airport wondering what to do next. You call a number that was given to you and there is no answer. Your mind already starts wandering and you have that little bit of anxiety in your gut. You try calling a few minutes later again and still no answer. You are now looking at your wife and the kids wondering if you screwed up.

That scenario already is a total nightmare and one that we would never want to put our guests through.

Whether you answer on the third call, their trip in your city is already starting off on a bad foot. You wouldn't do this to your family and you certainly cannot let this happen to your guests, ever.

We provide our guests with a toll free number or a 1-800 number to call upon their arrival. This is extremely important because when they first arrive in the city or a country, they may not have the correct currency and certainly may not have any change to call you from a payphone. Their cell phones are usually roaming and its costs an arm and a leg to call from a cell phone. The easier you can make it on the guest to call you from the airport, the easier everything will go.

There may be times when you cannot answer the phone right away. You must explain this to the guest ahead of time, while they are still at home. You must let them know not to worry and that if you cannot get to the phone at that particular time, ask them to try again in five or ten minutes. Ask them to leave a detailed message so that at least you know who called and that they arrived safely. I cannot state enough how important it is to answer their calls when they first call. That will be their first relief upon arrival, to hear your voice again upon landing. They will then know that they have arrived, are safe and will be at their condo in a matter of no time.

Ask them how their trip was, be sure to know who they are travelling with. If they are travelling with children, ask them how the kids are doing. Listen to what you are being told. Are the kids tired or hungry? Is the wife nervous? You want to guests to be excited about visiting your country or your city and it is your job to make sure everyone is happy. If the airline gave them bad service, be sympathetic and assure them that from now on their trip will be great! The guests just want to be assured that by staying with you, they will be taken care of.

If there are children visiting, prepare ahead of time for them. Most kids after travelling do get tired and cranky and anything you can do to help out the parents with the kids will be a huge help. If we know that children will be arriving, make sure to know the ages of the children and have the television set to an appropriate channel. This will help the parents out a lot by having the kids out of the way while they get settled into the condo, chat with you about directions, rules or otherwise get familiar with the suite. It's also nice to have a welcome package for the kids that consists of a drink box (not grape as you know this will end up on the carpets) a healthy snack and a small toy. This should take care of any hungry kids, any thirsty kids or kids that are need their attention focused anywhere but on their parents.

What you don't want is a situation where a family arrives with a bunch of cranky kids. You are busy trying to talk to the parents, explaining how everything works when the rascals are pulling on their parents whining about how hungry they are. Anyone with kids understands this and it makes for a less than fun filled family holiday. These little items make a huge difference and the parents will appreciate the few minutes of quiet time that you have given them. It is a tremendous difference, believe me.

Prior to a guest leaving their country, it's a great idea to have their flight information. Advise the guests that you like to have this information in case there is a delay in their travel plans, they won't need to worry about us not knowing. There are numerous flight trackers and you should check their flight status before leaving to meet with them. This will give you actual time of their flights, whether the flight is delayed or landed on time. If you do not check and leave to go and meet them at the suite, you will only become frustrated when you are waiting for two or three hours because their flight was delayed. Although you may feel frustrated because you wonder if they will even show up, imagine how they would be feeling with a full family travelling, knowing their flights are delayed by three hours and have no way to reach you to tell you. Life is so much easier when you have this information on hand, actually use it and the guests will feel better as well, knowing that you are aware of what is happening.

So now you have your family or your super guests in town! This is very exciting as you finally get to meet the people that you have been corresponding with. Everyone is nervous and excited at the same time. Make sure that you are aware of how they are arriving, is it transit, rental car, taxi or driver service? Do not just wait for them to arrive, make sure you are aware of how they are arriving and let them know that you are there every step of the way. Offer advice on the best form of transportation.

Our favorite is our driver service that we have hooked up with for our guests. The guests are able to speak with their driver prior to leaving and make all the arrangements directly with the driver. This way, they know who is picking them up, where they are to be picked up from, and the driver is familiar with where the condos are and can take the guests directly there. In Vancouver, the driver service is not much more than a taxi, is much bigger, cleaner and more luxurious than a taxi and with our driver service, you don't need to worry about how much the fare is because it's always the same every time. We know the driver and life has been much easier than trying to speak with lost taxi cab drivers who don't know where they are going, while the fare is ticking.

If the guest is renting a car, be sure to ask them if they need directions. A simple, "Okay, see you at the condo" from a guest representative is simply not good enough. Know the best route to the condo and offer it to them. Advise them of laws or bylaws about your particular city. Some cities have laws where you can't talk on your cell phones while driving, for instance. Advise them of that law before they get a ticket. Advise them of rush hours as well which would allow them to stop somewhere first and not have to battle traffic.

Upon their arrival at the building, please meet them outside the garage and guide them in. I don't really like how guests have to find parking outside and find the building, go in to do paperwork and then have to go back and get their car. This is a full service company and you certainly wouldn't do this with your family, so please don't do this with the guests. Meet them at the gate of the garage and lead them all the way to their parking stall.

I used to like to run all the way to their stall. Not only did the guests find it funny but they didn't have to drive around in circles, very slowly, watching you walk. This could make them fall asleep! Once they arrived at their spot, I would joke that its part of the company fitness program and that was the cardio portion. The weight portion was to help them with their luggage! Most people insist on carrying the big or heavy luggage. I always insisted on carrying the biggest luggage and was good at doubling up on all the bags. Have them carry the least amount of luggage as possible, after all, they are the ones tired from travelling, not you having to wait for them. I know I don't carry any of my own luggage at a five star hotels, so why should they?

The guests will arrive at the suite, knowing exactly how to get to their garage, where exactly their parking is, where the elevators are and know exactly how to get to their suite. This is a huge difference from having to drive around a big city looking for the entrance to their garage, then looking for a numbered stall. After lugging the luggage out of your car, there is nothing more frustrating than having to find the entrance to the elevator. Trying to figure out how to use the elevator system might get frustrating as well. It makes a huge difference if the guests are helped all the way.

Once at the suite, please be an example and take your shoes off and ask the guests to do the same. These are not hotels but they are someone's condo, someone's investment. Make sure to not only have the courtesy to take care of the suites as if they are your own but also encourage the guests to do the same. As you would have arrived prior to the guests, the heat and lights should all be on for when they enter. Ask the guests which bags and luggage would belong to which bedroom and bring their luggage into the bedroom for them. I like to put the bags or luggage right into the closet if it fits, so that the condo looks kept at all times. It doesn't look very good when you have a bunch of luggage piled up by the front door so have the suite organized the best you can so that the luggage is put away and they can enjoy the condo right away.

This would be the time to explain how everything works in the suite including the television, which is the most common phone call you would get that they don't know how it works. Explain how to use the phone as they would dial differently in a different country. Of course, local people you will not need to explain this to. Be sure to go over the internet and any passwords that they would require to log on. It's also nice to point out where extra towels are kept as we had some phone calls with irate guests claiming we didn't provide enough towels. After asking if they looked under the sink, they realized they were there the whole time. Save them the frustration and embarrassment and gently point these small items out to them.

Be sure to go over the location of where they are. It's nice to know where the closest 24 hour convenience stores or restaurants are. Some guests that travel from other countries in different parts of the world may still feel as if they are in a different time zone. It's nice to know where you can get a snack at 5am or any other odd time. Point out the grocery stores, restaurants, malls, etc. We like to leave small maps or discount coupons inside the suite that you could get from the tourist office. Leave this for the guests as it's very useful to them.

Before leaving, make sure that the guests are comfortable, have all of their questions answered and remind them to call anytime should they require anything at all. If they have any questions that require you to get back to them, be sure to write this down! I like to send an email or call the office and leave a voice message so that there are at least two staff members that are aware of their concerns. As some guests may stay as little as three or four days, it is urgent to resolve any issues by the next day. Do not ever advise a guest that you will take care of a broken item as soon as they leave in case something else comes up but be sure to take care of it right away.

We also like to have small brochures or coupons, samples, etc. to places that may be of interest to them. Depending on the guest, we have different items, brochures and coupons with us at all times. Upon getting to know them, we offer them certain items that are of particular interest to them. We used to have general coupons within the suite binder, but we found that these were not very personal and often overlooked. When offered directly to a guest as if it's only for that guest, not only does it mean so much more, but they then feel that they are really being looked after.

During a Guests' Stay

You have worked really hard up to this point to get a guest to your suite. The days that they are with you will be important ones. Do not rest for even a second thinking that your work is now over because they have paid and arrived. This could be the most important part of the job.

Guests will call for all sorts of reasons. This is the time to be on call; to be on standby. They will call because one light bulb has burned out and they would like that changed. They could use one extra towel, how soon could you come over? How does the television work? They can't get on the internet and they need help.

Yes, some of these requests can be frustrating. I, myself, had a similar experience.

> ➤ Staying at a hotel, I could not get the lamp to work at all. I finally gave up and called maintenance to bring me a new light bulb. Trying to be helpful, I took the light bulb at the front door and advised maintenance that I would just change it myself. Being in the hospitality industry, I did not want to bother them any more than I had to. I changed the bulb and still nothing. I debated whether I really even needed the light. After some thought, I confirmed that I did need

that light after all. While on the phone with maintenance for the second time, asking them to come back because the lamp still wasn't working, my nine-year-old son sat across from me with the plug from the lamp asking, "Do you think it would work better if this was plugged in?"

The receptionist heard this on the phone. All I could reply was, "Please do not speak of this to anyone!" We both laughed but I felt like an idiot! We all make these minor mistakes and it can be very frustrating for another party.

We start to solve these minor issues by using preventative measures. Of course a light bulb can go out shortly after we have left. How many times have we turned on a light and it just went out, these things do happen. For smaller lamps and easy to reach places, guests would rather just change their own light bulb than have to call and wait for someone to come over. Make sure to keep a couple of spare light bulbs underneath the kitchen sink so that they can change the small lights themselves. These days some lights are so fancy that you need to find that one special light specifically for a certain lamp. These are usually built in and although we do buy these in bulk, there are so many lights that require many different bulbs that you may, from time to time, have to go out, purchase the bulb and then change it. If you only have the one condo, then be sure to buy several at the same time to at least save yourself the time of going to purchase more.

We keep a list of all of the complaints that come in so that we can work to make sure those same complaints don't happen again. It would be a major problem and issue if the same problem kept coming up. After a few complaints like that, it would definitely be something that you are doing wrong, not the guests' complaints.

We advise the guests ahead of time of what towels to expect. Although most people are honest, there will be a few that slip through the cracks. Our rates are based on the number of people we have in the suite. If they would like to have more people, we do allow that, but there is an extra charge for that. Don't forget, the more people staying in the suite, the more water they would be using, the more lights and appliances, etc. These costs do add up so you want to be clear up front what the rates include. We make it very clear that there are towels and guest amenities for four people. We do offer more towels, linens, sheets, pillows, etc., but that does come with an extra cost. Not that the guests would be dishonest, but the ones that are coming with 5, 6 or 7 people often plan on just complaining about not enough towels or that they are cold and need more blankets or extra sheets. Unfortunately, this is to avoid paying the extra person cost and we are very clear on what the rate includes. This is another reason why it's a good idea when at the suite, to go over and show them where everything is for those four people.

Please be sure to have housekeeping readily available or be able to go back to re-clean a suite immediately. The next day is usually too late as the guests would be very upset and no matter how well you clean the suite, they will only remember the dirty suite. One hotel I checked into in Las Vegas, had hand prints along the top of the headboard in the bedroom. Although housekeeping came in to re-clean the handprints, I will never forget those, nor do I ever want to stay there again. Yes, I am very aware of what goes on in Vegas, I just didn't want to see any evidence of it in my suite. The guests may forgive, but they will never forget.

We have also seen guests that have made up complaints just to receive a discount. They have complained that a suite was dirty but do not want anyone to come over and clean. They didn't notice this upon their check in but they are noticing it the next day. They simply want a discount and not a re-clean. It is hard to prove that a suite is dirty when the guest was checked in and the suite was clean. It's also difficult to prove that after they have already stayed for 24 hours. We do have a policy that a suite will be cleaned again if they find it dirty, but that they will not receive a discount for that of any sort. What we will offer is a discount for the next stay. I have seen this happen at other hotels as well, with people I know and I am very embarrassed to even be seen with them. Again, with policies in place ahead of time of what we offer in these events, it does bring the complaints down quite a bit. Yes, some suites will actually be dirty, but at that time, those people will want to suite cleaned, not left dirty.

> We had one guest that checked in at 2pm at our office, drove half an hour to her condo and called us at 4pm. She was irate

because when they arrived, their suite was dirty and they had to go out and purchase $100 worth of cleaning products, go back to the condo and scrub the whole condo for two hours! They demanded a discount! Now, someone who wants a discount would not spend $100 on cleaning products. What could they have possibly purchased for that much money? Why would they even spend their vacation shopping for cleaning products and scrubbing an apartment for 2 hours when they were only at the condo for an hour? Everything about this story didn't make sense. They wouldn't even provide us with the receipt so we could reimburse them for the cleaning products; all they wanted was a discount.

Another key person that you will require on call would be the handy man. Great if you can do this work yourself, but it's important to have a handyman on call in case something does break down. Again, some guests are only there for three or four days, it would be unreasonable for them to wait three days to have something like a toilet fixed. It is important to have an agreement with a handy man that they would arrive within 24 hours at the most.

This part alone is another important reason to have a company look after your property instead of doing this yourself. The investment companies usually have someone on staff at all times that is able to arrive at a condo the same day. The guests' experience will depend on the efficiency of looking after their concerns and nothing can ruin a vacation faster than having to wait two days for a plumber. It is very important to have someone available that can come right away.

Just before a guest leaves, give them a courtesy call or email to see how their stay was and to see if there is anything that they require before their departure. Do they require airport drop off or directions to the airport? Do you need to meet them at the suite in order for them to checkout or can they just leave the keys. Most people don't remember the checkout procedure although it's written in the book, they may not want to read the guide all over again. It's nice to give them a call with checkout instructions.

The phone call is also a fantastic friendly reminder of their checkout time. Before we had this courtesy call, we would have housekeeping show up at the checkout time just to find people still sleeping. We had another guest due to check in in about two hours, so you can see the frustration at that hour. We have also heard many excuses, from "We forgot" to "No one told us" to "I didn't get enough sleep because we had to listen to sirens all night long." We do laugh at the last one only because these people come from quiet towns to a big city, stay right in downtown Vancouver on a Friday or Saturday night and don't expect to hear any sirens? Then it wouldn't be a city. If people ask about noise levels, we also tell them that by staying downtown, there are sirens. Living in a big city you won't notice them as much, but if you come from a small town where the town ambulance only gets called out once a month, I could see how someone wouldn't get any sleep on a Friday night, right downtown where all the action is. You will get these city sounds, especially if you leave your windows open!

So, don't forget to give them that friendly phone call with a gentle reminder about their checkout time. If you must leave a voice message, please do so, along with a follow-up email. We do have a fine if you check out past the checkout time, if you do not have it arranged beforehand. It is a big frustration when the schedule is made for the day only to arrive at a suite and guests are still there. By the time you reorganize the schedule and get to the other suite, you lose a good hour of your day. It's especially important when there are guests checking in at a specific time as they do not like to wait to check in, not even for half hour. Trust me on that one.

We don't fine for the purpose of extra revenue but we do fine for the purpose of the guest's knowing that their checkout time is very important. We are accommodating however we can be with those times as long as they have it pre-arranged. Since we have implemented the fine, we have noticed a decrease in late, non-pre-arranged checkouts. Since the fine, it rarely happens which makes for a much smoother day. Of course, the guests absolutely have the option to check out later, just as long as it is confirmed ahead of time. Nothing is as great as smooth operations!

It probably goes without saying, to check for any items that the guests have left behind. We also have spare freezer bags so that we can put the item in the bag and label it with the guests' name and suite number. There was one time where we were able to call the guest while they were still at the airport and speed over to the airport to meet them with their items. They were very grateful and of course, the staff was delighted that we were able to find the item, call the guest and meet them before their flight left. Lesson learned was to call the guest immediately after discovering anything forgotten in the suite, not after you return to the office or home.

Within three days of a guests' checkout, we send out a short survey to see how their stay went. Each survey should be tailored to your own business needs and to see how you can better serve the customer next time. There are a few companies out there that even provide free surveys, so be sure to Google them and find one that will work with your condo or your business. Be sure to read these surveys and look for ways to improve. Your goal should be to have better and better scores every time. The guests' will also know that you care for their opinion even after they have paid and left. A lot can be learned from these surveys, they are free, so be sure to use them!

Every person's job within a company has great importance and influence over the next person's job. The following is a letter that went out to all staff to stress how important each and every single person is that is a part of our team:

Working for Malibu Investments is like being a family or a team. We cannot have a one person team or a one person family. Every single person's job affects another person's job as well. Your particular job affects me, my personal family, the other staff, the other staff's families, the guests and the owners. Your job is not insignificant but is a very important part of the team. Without you specifically, the entire company could not operate.

Let me introduce you to each person's job and how it affects you:

Marketing Department: *This is the department that makes the ads. This person adds the photos, researches and writes the descriptions, posts ads on numerous websites every single day, researches the competition to make sure our ads and prices are the best, updates rates, etc. Without this person's job, we would not have any guests for us to do the rest of our jobs.*

Guest Services/Sales: *After all of the hard work of the marketing department, Guest Services now has a job. Guest Services is the department that the guests speak or email with. They have to have the knowledge of the suites, the area, and the guest's needs and be able to overcome any objections that a potential guest may have. They need to be fast and flexible and in case a particular suite is not available, they must be able to think quickly and be able to offer them something else. We all depend on this person as well and hope that they make the sale so that all of us can continue to work. Once guests are here, this person must answer any questions that they have about the suites,* *the area and our policies. Without this person, none of us would have jobs.*

Housekeeping: *Thank goodness for the hard work of the marketing team and the sales team, housekeeping now has work. One of the very first things that guests notice when they arrive is the cleanliness of the suite. They will notice everything! The guests want their sheets to be clean, beds made looking lovely, towels folded neatly, no dust anywhere in the suite, dishes clean and put away, the suite smelling nice, etc. Without this persons job, guest services would be receiving unhappy calls and would need to start giving out discounts and earning the company less money. Marketing would then need to look out for bad publicity or negative comments on websites. Without clean suites, we wouldn't have any product to offer. The entire product and service is based on clean and well equipped suites. Without this, the rest of us wouldn't have jobs.*

If you take out any of these jobs, the entire company would fail and could not exist. Every single person's job is dependent on another's and is important and vital to the livelihood of the rest of the company.

We all ask each other to take every single action of your job extremely seriously as many people depend on it. Housekeeping must have the suite in impeccable condition so that the efforts of marketing and sales are rewarded. Guest Services ensures that the guests have all of their questions answered and they receive something of value so that the efforts of marketing and the work of housekeeping don't go to waste. Marketing, the rest of the team depends on you to make the phone ring and the emails to be received. Without your efforts, we wouldn't have guests to fill the suites with.

The owners trust us with their investment properties and trust that we deliver an acceptable amount of rent to them every month. These properties are their livelihoods and their families depend on the jobs that we do. Our entire company is based on referrals and for every one owner that we let down, there could be 10 more that we could have been referred to.

We all depend on each other and our company is only as good as our weakest link. Every single job here is extremely important and every person is equally is important.

As part of a job well done recognition, the company had sent one of the staff to Las Vegas for an all-expenses paid trip. I enjoy randomly rewarding people and enjoy surprising them as well. Of course, the trip was not all fun and games and an afternoon was spent discussing company policies and procedures and how to better our services. This of course happened in the conference room which was an outdoor private cabana in front of a private pool with lunch and bottled water. This was followed by a spa after a grueling day of meetings.

Another part of this "conference" was a surprise event that I entitled, "Exceeding Customer Expectations." This was actually a Cirque du Soleil show which I wanted to show the employee about how everyone's job is important to another person's job and how we all depend on each other. Here is what I wrote and sent out to the company after the show:

- Exceeding Customer Expectations

  We had the pleasure of watching a show put on by Cirque de Soleil in Las Vegas, during our annual business conference. Although the show was spectacular, behind the scenes it is a business. This business has made the owner one of the richest people in Canada and on the top 100 wealthiest people in the world!

  The entire team consists of numerous people. There are the stage performers, the people that the audience gets to see. There are the people behind the stage, such as lighting, sound, props, costumes, directors, etc. Even further behind the scenes and probably nowhere near the building at the time of the show are people such as marketing, accounting, promoters, executives, etc. The entire show would not work without all of the staff depending on each other, and they do depend on each other.

  Imagine doing the show and not getting paid because accounting didn't feel like going to work? Imagine trying to do a stage show if lighting decides to quit in the middle of the show? What about the person playing the music, what about if he didn't feel like coming to work? The show certainly wouldn't work without every single person being involved and everyone is equally as important throughout the entire company. That is what makes a company and that is what makes that show such a huge success!

The show itself, I'm quite sure is exactly the same show, every time, night after night. I doubt that one show would be different from another show. Every single person does the same thing, at the exact time, every time. I doubt if someone "forgot" to wear their costume or "forgot" their shoes or head piece. I doubt the Maria is new and she dances differently than everyone else or that Susie tried her best but it's her first day on the show so she wasn't quite sure where exactly to step on the stage. Although this time, she didn't catch the person falling out of the sky, she will next time, for sure.

Every person's job is exactly the same, with clear and precise directions on how to do every single step, down to the last second. One mistake and the whole show suffers. We were lucky enough to witness a mistake because a performer was off by one inch! The performer did not land on top of the other performer as planned. Although clearly a mistake, the entire team repositioned quickly and performed the trick as it was to be originally performed. The entire audience was forgiving simply because everything else was that fantastic, but more so because the performer quickly recovered and performed the trick as planned. The audience was not only forgiving but delighted that no one got hurt and the show went on!

Business is exactly the same way. Every team member depends on everyone else. In the case of the miscalculated jump, no one singled out that one particular person, it was the entire show that we speak of. It was miscalculated by everyone. If there is one mistake within a company, the entire company suffers because of it. It is extremely important that every single person does their job with precision so that the entire company looks good as a whole.

Every step is calculated and very accurate. It is done the exactly the same way, every single time. This way, every time we go to this show, we know that we would see precisely the same show. The show starts at the exact same time, every time. The costumes are the same ones, every time. When discussing the show with other people and viewing it in a different city or even country, it is the same show, every single time.

Our company needs to run the same way. We need to depend on each other like they depend on each other. We all want to be confident that we all get paid by the 5th or 20th, on time, every single time. The owners want their checks by the 15th, on time, every single time. The guest services are to answer calls between 9am and 5pm every single time, every day of the week, every time. The suites are to be cleaned the same way, every single time. The guest's invoices need to be accurate, every single time. This way, when we depend on each other, we all look good no matter who did the actual job. In the end, we will have happy customers who know that they can count on us to receive the same great service, on time, every single time.

We should also provide a little extra, just like we had the funny old guy before the show provide us with a bit of an extra show, before the actual show.

That was my report to the whole company to demonstrate how we all depend on each other. I wish I could have taken everyone to the show as it's a great demonstration of how dependent we are on each other.

Chapter Summary

- ✓ Offer an immaculately clean suite
- ✓ Have an easy check in process for the guest

- ✓ Offer a toll free phone number to the guests
- ✓ Show the guests around the building as well as the condo
- ✓ Follow up with a guest during their stay
- ✓ Respond to all complaints immediately

CHAPTER 7
Policies & Systems

Every company or business as well as individual people managing their own properties, must have policies as well as systems in place. For individuals, it's important to have your policies or a manual on how to do things, written down and kept somewhere accessible. Imagine if something unfortunate happened where you were not able to tend to your business for a couple of days? It is important to have someone else who knows where the manual is and how to take care of your business even for a few days. Guests and tenants are not very forgiving if you disappear for a few days, no matter what the reason.

A business must have a manual and policies with its systems written down. The entire point of creating and running a business is being able to slowly walk away from it where you are not needed, however the business can thrive on its own. They are like children; the most amount of work is at the beginning where someone needs to tend to them 24 hours a day. As they slowly grow up (actually, they grow up too fast) we teach them one skill at a time such as eating and going to the bathroom, etc. After a while, they automatically do these things completely on their own, they don't need to be told when to do it, how to do it, etc. But it does take up to two years to teach them to go to the bathroom on their own.

Your business or the managing company will be the same way. There is a lot of work at the beginning where the owner is the secretary, the plumber, the cleaner, the accountant, etc. When I first started, I was the one cleaning the suites, answering all of my own phone calls, bringing my laptop with me to the suites when I cleaned them and stopped in the middle of a clean to take a reservation. My vehicle was my mobile office, where half was dedicated to cleaning products and the other half was the office. The systems that I had set up were to accommodate my mobile cleaning as well as the office portion of my vehicle. There would be a number of times when I would have to pull over to answer questions, have a wireless router attached to my laptop so that I can open up the reservation system and email the guests, a wireless attached to my head, etc.

Upon arriving at home, I would process all reservations, work on the marketing, call and follow-up on the guests, do the accounting and be on standby at all times in case a guest had some inquiries. If there was anything that needed to be fixed, I would be the one to go over and fix something. If I didn't know how, I would Google the solution and then fix it myself. When you first start out or are managing your own property, it could get very expensive to hire a maintenance person as there isn't much profit. This would be another great reason to have a managing company look after it as the maintenance should be less expensive if they do it than if you do it yourself.

As you go along and build your portfolio, it is important to have these policies written down. When you are working on your own, this shouldn't take too long to do. Imagine if you had an emergency to tend to and had to drop off your phone, keys, all business related items with a friend. This manual would be a step by step guide on what to do. It must be detailed enough so that they won't have any questions in case you are not there to answer them. Have the heading very clear in sections such as marketing, customer service (answering calls), cleaning, keys, etc. Have the tabs clearly displayed so that the person looking after your things doesn't have to read the entire manual just to have one question answered.

We have several manuals for every single department. A sample of some of our policies are included at the end to show you how detailed they must be. Please, please do not assume that what is obvious to you will be obvious to everyone else. Also, you must have a system to be able to verify if something was done. Here are a few examples of our housekeeping department. You may also want to review the complete list at the back of the book which we have provided.

Our manual explains the housekeeping procedure from the minute they get to the door. Although we assume that a guest has already checked out by their checkout time, there will be one or two incidents of where the guests either "didn't know about the checkout time," or "we slept in because we didn't sleep last night because of all the city noise in the middle of the night that you didn't tell us about," or any other excuse that we have already heard in the past. We do have a policy that if they do not checkout on time, there are additional charges. We will go over this further in the contracts section.

Housekeeping is required to knock on the door first to ensure that there is no one in the suite. Upon entering the suite, they are to have a look to ensure that the guests have already left. They look for things such as shoes, personal belongings, etc. The best way we can tell if they have already checked out is by looking on the floor as the guests are required to take the front door key off the keychain, lock the door and slide the key under the door. Therefore, when we open the door and see the key on the ground, we know that the guests have checked out. The guests are instructed to leave the rest of the keys on the kitchen counter (garage door openers, elevator fobs, etc.). If the housekeeper does not see the key on the ground and can't find it anywhere, they are to call the office immediately. If they do find the key and the rest of the keys on the kitchen counter, then they are to put the key back on to the keychain and not mix that up with the other keys.

Although you will notice that we do have that policy written down, step by step, like Housekeeping for Dummies, oddly enough these instructions weren't very clear to some of the housekeepers.

> One incident happened where the housekeeper picked up the key and put it back on her keychain (the housekeepers set of keys). She then proceeded to do her work, etc., and return all keys at the end of the day. When the next guest checked in, we received a call at midnight saying that they keys that she has do not work in the door. I remember thinking how is that even possible? Upon investigating further, it turned out that the housekeeper had picked up the key on the floor, put in on her own keychain instead of the guest keychain and the guest was issued the guest keys without the actual front door key on it while the cleaner had two front door keys on her own keychain. I remember thinking, how could someone have gotten that wrong? What kind of a ding-a-ling does that? At the end of the day, as the business owner, you are responsible for the policies and systems that you create and I had to accept the fact that there was something wrong with my system, although it was clearly written down. We have now amended that policy so that instead of writing down "one set of keys" we now have to write down exactly what that is. For example, "one set of keys: one front door key, one building front door key, one garage door opener." This way, when they keys are returned, we confirm that actual keys that are to be on the one set of keys. Again, do not assume that people

can read and will follow your directions and instructions, even though they are obvious to you and me. At the end of the day, the guest calls and yells at you, not the cleaner. Meanwhile, the cleaner is sleeping soundly at home, without a care in the world.

The other incident that we had was when housekeeping or the guest representative decided to make his or her own rules without even consulting anyone else. Although our policies on checking out are clear, such as leave the keys in the suite, we had one cleaner who I think tried to break every rule we had. She gave out her personal number for the guests to call her directly, which they did. They asked about what to do with the keys when they checkout. We do have an information booklet inside the suite with these directions but failing that, they can of course call the office to find out, it's what we are here for. It is also included in the contract that they sign that they keys must be returned immediately after checkout otherwise there will be a $500 fine if the keys are not returned right at checkout. The guest representative instead gave the guests her personal number which is against company policy. The guests called to ask about what to do with the keys when they leave. She had instructed them to leave one full set inside the suite, lock up with the other set of keys, take those keys home with them back to wherever they came from, provided her personal home address to them and told them to send them back when they got home.

PROFITS IN REAL ESTATE RENTALS

When I first heard about that, I thought that the staff was joking with me. I was seriously laughing at first, thinking, "Ya, right, someone would do that . . ." It ended up being true! I was speechless!! So now, we had no keys to get inside the suite at all, we had guests coming to check in and we had another guest that still had a set of keys to the suite. This is a big problem for several reasons. Not to mention the obvious reasons why staff cannot give out their home address to guests, but we cannot have two guests with keys to the same suite at the same time. We don't know for sure if those guests really went home and worst case scenario, they could wait until a guest checks in and use those same keys to access the suite and rob them. I know, you may be thinking that I am being paranoid but after being in this business, the only way to conduct business is from the worst case scenario point of view and then everything else runs smoothly.

At the end of the day, we had to call in a locksmith to not only give us access to our own suite but to change locks on the condo as we cannot be certain that the guests are not still in town with a set of keys. Safety first, especially when it comes to guests! The charges of the locksmith were billed right back to the housekeeper, who is an independent contractor and did not do her job according to our policies. I keep telling staff that when in doubt simply call and ask. Do not make your own executive decisions unless you are an executive yourself and are authorized to make these decisions. It took me a while to get over that incident.

Again, we are back to what did I do wrong where my policies and systems failed me? The guests have signed a contract that says that they must return keys right after they checkout but they could have understood that to mean as soon as we get home we will mail them back. It is also written in the book inside the suite, but this information could have been hard to find or better yet, who actually reads these books while on holiday anyways? We also have a guest representative who should be familiar with our policies and can guide our guests to the correct answer. Clearly, the representative was also not clear on these policies, even though she can make her own decisions. Either way, this section had to be reviewed to ensure that the next new employee would not have ever made the same mistake. Again, do not assume that just because it's written and you understand it and it seems so obvious, that these things will not still happen. It's all a work in progress, fine tuning the systems that you have.

At the beginning, we would also send out what needed to be done on the day that it needed to be done. For example, Monday morning you have a look to see who is checking in and out. Make your notes or printout, etc., and head off for the day. We had an issue once where a guest called to say, "We are here!" We thought, you are where, as we didn't have anyone checking in that day. "We are at the condo for our check in today," they told us. The staff looked at each other wondering what the heck is going on. As soon as we looked in our reservation system, it was clear. It was written right there, in the calendar, that we had a guest checking into a certain suite and in that same suite, we had someone checking out. How the heck did we miss that? I cannot even begin to describe the panic that we all felt! The suite was not even cleaned yet and the guests were already there.

We have since changed that policy again so that a weekly schedule goes out at the same time every week for the entire week. This way, we can see up to a week in advance what we have coming up. We have a big white board where every Friday we have this cleared and rewritten. The day before, whoever is on shift for the following day, also gets an email with the schedule for the next day. This way, if there is anything that needs tending to or needs to be purchased, it can even be done the day before and not the morning of. We also email out a final schedule the morning of work. This would serve as the third notice of our schedule, eliminating what happened that day. Or is it?

Even with my foolproof new system, this happened again! How the heck can this even happen? What I found was that an employee would simply cut and paste the original schedule and email it the night before. In the morning they would cut and paste the same email and send it out again. So, if there was a mistake the first time, this same mistake was repeated for every single email. It ended up that the schedule was only checked once as this employee was too lazy, yes, I said lazy, to physically check the schedule herself for accuracy and email her own schedule. She simply took what the other staff had emailed, copied and pasted her email and sent that out. It goes to show you that again, although the instructions are clearly written and they seem obvious to everyone, someone will take that system and make it into their own, therefore causing problems in the end.

We are currently using a fantastic reservation system called reservation key (www.reservationkey.com). This system is not very expensive at all, about $15 per month. You really should be using this system right from the very beginning. It is very easy to use, fantastic guest contact database that keeps track of your guests, their stay, how much they spend, how many reservations they have had with you, what they like or enjoy doing, etc. You can color code your reservations to numerous fields such as a quote, reserved, checked out, maintenance, not available or any other field that you would find necessary. The support is great as well. We usually get a response to any questions that we have almost immediately. They have even been so good as to make a special field that we really found we needed. I can't see us ever using anything else. For the money you spend, you get so much value. I love this system!

I find that most of our problems are actually a result of the policies not being followed, even though they are written down, reminded, discussed, etc. There always has to be a check up of the work that was done and you cannot assume that the notes you give someone are actually being followed. They may also be followed for a certain amount of time but at some point, they make their own rules, make their own decisions or deem that it's not actually necessary to follow those rules. That's when problems start and can turn into huge problems quickly!

With every rule or policy, it must be written in plain English so that even non-English speaking people can understand. This must also accompany an explanation of why we do things as well as the consequences of what happens if certain procedures are not followed. We have had several incidences where employees knew the rules but made up their own as they went along. There was even one where things were explained through a conversation, we then emailed her the basic instructions, and then, after a third time of not following those instructions we had a meeting to go over everything again. This was followed up by an email and we then had the same problem arise for a fourth time. If you have any suggestions on how to cut down on getting through to people for the first time, please email me! At this time, an employee contract is the best way clearly set expectations, have them read everything, discuss it, sign it and hopefully follow it.

We were having several issues of an employee constantly giving out her personal number as well as her personal email address. There are reasons why an employee cannot hand out their personal numbers or email addresses. The first one is that the access to that information is limited, meaning only that one person has access to that information. For example, let's say that a guest has arrived early and they call the employees direct number to say they have arrived early and are already waiting at the condo. Of course, if that employee is away from their phone where they can't answer, that guest will leave a message on that personal phone and no one will be able to access that until the employee retrieves her messages. Even worse,

I use the proverbial "worst case scenario and you get hit by a bus," there would be no way for anyone to know that a guest has arrived early if that phone never gets answered or the messages never get checked.

Having a central phone system is most effective and allows a guest to call and speak directly with someone. At our company, a guest would call and be able to speak to someone right away. This way, we can call the guest services representative and advise them that a guest has arrived early and see if they can get over there right away. If that person can't, we can then call someone else to see who is available to get there right away. If the guest calls and no one answers the call right away, their message is a digital message that is emailed out to the staff on duty and several people at the same time have access to that message. That way, if the first receptionist is already on a call, someone else can quickly start calling to see who is available to do a check in right away. It's a much better system than having an employee who is the only one that can access that voice message.

Another reason we require all calls to go through the central phone system is that we have a database of all calls, call logs and messages that come in. There is nothing worse than a guest saying they left a message and there is no record of it because the company cannot access someone's personal voice mail or that employee "accidentally" deleted it. For any discrepancies, we also have to be able to go back to all emails and voice messages when we are investigating a complaint or extra charges or for any other reason. All calls, call logs, voice mail, etc., must be in one central system. If any employee quits and you need access to that information for any future reference, not only will they be unwilling to hand that over but I doubt that they would have saved any voice messages from past guests for any length of time.

For privacy reasons, all personal and contact information must stay with the company. Their names, phone numbers and email address, must all remain on company phones, company emails, etc. This information is the property of the company or the individual who manages their own properties and cannot stay on anyone else's phone. There needs to be a strict policy about this and there needs to be consequences for breaching this rule. We manage high end properties and if Brad Pitt and Angelina Jolie come to stay with us, they certainly don't want to be receiving personal calls or emails from staff. They absolutely must have their private and confidential information kept just that. Simply imagine the worst that could happen and protect yourself from that point of view. If any staff takes their phone number or their email and passes it along to someone else, who in turns contacts them and it does get back to you or your company that it leaked, you will be liable for all expenses they may have to go through to have that information changed. It can be very costly, not to mention, a very bad reputation that you will be left with and you can definitely forget about getting a referral from them. Privacy and the protection of their information is high priority for them.

CHAPTER 8
Freedom from Real Estate

When I first set up my business and my company, I was thinking about how I would want the company to run when I retired. When I retire, I still want to own a huge portfolio of real estate but I don't want to have anything do to with the day-to-day operations of real estate. I want to travel, spend time with my family and do all the things that I would want to do without any responsibilities. Of course, it would be nice to have all the monthly income simply deposited into my account without me even having to go to a bank to as much as much as deposit a check. Life would be grand!

Real estate makes money in three different ways when it's a revenue property. The asset normally appreciates in value every year, if there is a mortgage on the property, this will get paid down every month which will increase the equity month over month. Finally, when positioned properly, you will have positive cash flow every single month. I get excited about the cash flow assets without a mortgage on the property. This is what we should be striving for. Although today there may be a mortgage on your property, that day will come when that mortgage is paid off and you are simply enjoying the full positive cash flow. This, in my opinion, is the best retirement plan that anyone can have. The freedom to count on yourself, as opposed to any company pension, stock market or any government pension.

The systems are set up so that if you are looking after another owner's property, it will work where the owners are not bothered whatsoever. You must be able to look after every single aspect of their property, from guest services, to cleaning and maintenance. The owners should enjoy simply receiving a check deposited directly into their account by a set date and not have any worries other than that. If you are looking after their property, it is your job to worry about every aspect and do not bother them while they are lying on a beach with a Mai Tai in their hand. You will not want to receive any phone calls about a leaking toilet when it's your turn to lay on the beach, so please don't bother them now.

A clear contract between the owners and the investment managers should be made so that all the little details are covered. Keep in mind that one day you will want to be the one laying on the beach so be quite clear on all the work that you will do for the owner. Include items such as marketing and advertising, cleaning, maintenance of the suite, guest services, privacy agreements, etc. Any maintenance issue that may result from the guest's fault should be covered by the guest. Make the owner aware that the owner will still be responsible for other maintenance such as their appliances, electrical, plumbing and other maintenance. Most owners have a maximum amount that they are willing to spend on such items. Discuss this ahead of time with them so that they are not bothered for maintenance work up to a certain amount. For example, they would be willing to spend up to $100 in one month for these items but anything over $100 they would like to be consulted first prior to the work being completed. Decided between the owner and yourself, what their maximum is before they would like to be contacted in regards to the maintenance work. This amount will be different for every owner, so be sure to have this included in their contract.

Before leaving on an extended holiday or simply leaving your property with a management company that specializes in short term rentals, be sure that the suite is in top shape. The entire suite should have good paint so that the guests don't complain that the walls need repainting, carpets should be shampooed or changed to hardwood flooring because it's less expensive to maintain than carpets. If you choose to keep carpets, expect to have these shampooed two to three times per year, which ends up costing in the area of $300 to $450 during the year. All dishes and cutlery should be a full set with perhaps an extra set somewhere in the suite. All furniture should be fairly new and definitely no stains, cracks or any sign of wear and tear. All appliances should be checked to make sure that they work properly and have a long economic life left.

Have all utilities on automatic payment such as gas or electricity, cable, internet and phone. Make sure that the company looking after your suite is named on the account so that they can call for technical support or trouble shooting. The last thing you want to know is that the cable company refused to help the guests or the staff because their name is not on the account. Some cable companies will keep you on hold for over an hour before you can even get through to them or to even speak with anyone. I don't know about you but this is the last thing I want to be doing during retirement, especially when I have already paid someone to do this for me and who is able and willing to do it. Make sure the company name is on the account so that they have access to this account and this way you won't have to be on hold for an hour while you are on your holiday.

When you have utilities that are on automatic payment, you will notice this amount fluctuates at times. Have something in the contract that you are willing to pay up to a certain amount for heat and hot water and anything above that must be paid by the guest. Although not every management company will agree to that, it's a good idea to ask. Ensure that the guests are aware that that the utilities are paid up to a certain amount and anything over this amount will be billed to them. This works well with guests that are staying longer than one billing cycle, however, unless your utility company can break down your utility bill to a daily rate, this amount will be difficult to monitor. If they management company is not willing to include this stipulation in the guests contract, do not ask the company to pay any extra as they don't have control over this amount. Find a solution to minimize this bill.

Be sure that the company has all of your contact information and especially an email where your statements will be sent. You should expect to receive a monthly statement with a breakdown of the number of guests as well as the rate they paid, all commissions and any deductions. You should not have deductions every month and you should not have a full month where there are no reservations.

Unless you have specified that your suite cannot be rented for less than a month, there should be some reservations during the month, every single month. That is the bonus of having short term rentals, is that you don't have to wait for an entire month to get a tenant or a guest. There should be someone staying in there at some point during the month. If you do have a one or three month minimum, then it would be reasonable to have a full month vacancy as these are harder to fill for short term rentals.

Please advise in writing to any strata companies, building manager home owners associations regarding who is looking after your property and that they are authorized to act on your behalf. What you don't want happening while laying on the beach is having a guest lose a key and the management company not being able to order another key or building fob without your written consent. What would be worse is if the building manager won't accept an email and expects something with your signature on it, and then faxed. I'm sorry, but

I do not want to get off my beach chair to go and look for paper to write something down, and then look for a fax machine. Meanwhile, the staff can't get in to clean a suite because they have to go through procedures in obtaining another key from the building manager who is waiting for your fax. Those people generally don't even work a full day and are gone home by 3pm. You have a guest waiting and of course, can't check in so they have to be relocated to a different suite and you have now lost that income. It's better to have the building managers and everyone else involved that someone else is to look after your affairs. At the end of the day, you simply want to receive your check directly into your account without any further worry than that.

Just think about for a moment how exciting retirement will be. Think of where you want to be and what you want to be doing. You will have a very nice portfolio of assets where you don't have to look after it but you get a check every single month. This is the dream that we are aiming for. You can stay there whenever you want or have your friends or family have somewhere nice to stay. You can also pass this investment along to your family where they can simply enjoy the monthly income without worrying about receiving a large inheritance and spending it all. The possibilities are endless. The work that you put into this now is definitely worth the reward in the end.

Chapter Summary

- ✓ Have a clear contract between yourself and the investment company
- ✓ Provide all contact information for the company
- ✓ Provide direct deposit information
- ✓ Ensure the suite is new, fairly new or upgraded
- ✓ Fully stocked with all dishes, cutlery, small appliances, etc.
- ✓ All furniture is in great condition
- ✓ All forms for building managers are handed in
- ✓ All utilities are on automatic payment
- ✓ Utility companies are aware of who is looking after your property and have access

CHAPTER 9

Gossip about the Author

Here is a little background on where I came from and how I came to be a real estate investor. Most people want to know how someone gets started, what their background was and how a regular person can also be a real estate investor. There will be some juicy gossip, so keep reading.

I purchased my first house when I was 18 years old. Ever since I can remember, I always liked money. My parents emigrated from Poland when I was 6 years old. I remember moving to Edmonton and living in a small apartment with my parents and younger sister. My sister's name is Agnieszka. It has absolutely no meaning to this book whatsoever except that she changed her name to Jamaica when she was fourteen years old and has been called Jamaica ever since. I don't think anyone knows her as Agnieszka anymore and she absolutely hates that name. So I thought I would share that only with my closest readers.

The four of us lived in this small apartment. Someone was telling me about empty pop bottles and how there is a place that will give you money for every pop bottle that I bring in. I thought this was odd because there were pop bottles all over the streets, everywhere. Being six years old, I was thinking, "How is that even possible? So this guy is telling me that I see money everywhere and no one wants to pick it up? No one wants free money? This is strange."

I did some investigating and sure enough, there was a bottle depot. This bottle depot is a place where you bring in all your empty pop and other bottles and they give you money. So I brought a couple of those in to see what happens. They took those bottles and gave me $0.25! Holy cow! I couldn't believe this. Those people actually gave me money for bottles. I was 6 years old, just came from Poland and probably didn't even speak English at that time and I already made twenty-five cents. This was too good to be true.

I brought in any cans or bottles that I could find in the neighborhood. I think I went there daily to get a couple of cents per day. For a kid, this was the best thing on earth. I would then go home and play with my coins, organize them and put them in neat little stacks. I would recount my money daily and be amazed that every single day, I had more and more money. I was so rich!

I had another idea! I live in an apartment building . . . I could help these people clean out their garbage! I wondered if this would work. I went to grab a shopping cart that is usually left at the front of the building and began going door to door on every floor. It's weird how I had no fear of anyone saying no to me. I had no fear of anything other than the excitement that if this works, I will be super rich! I couldn't knock on someone's door to ask for anything now if my life depended on it.

Off I went, knocking on doors. Once they answered, I simply said, "I'm here to help you pick up your garbage of bottles and cans." Everyone found something in their house that they thought was garbage and threw their empties into my cart. That cart was almost full not too long after I started. There was one guy that opened the door that had cases of beer bottles. I used my line on him and he said he didn't have any. I remember leaning over to point out that I see a huge case of empties and he actually said no to me. Thirty years later I still remember what a jerk he was!

I don't remember how much money I made that day or every week that I went to collect their bottles. I was the official bottle collector and went on the same days every week. Although I don't remember the exact amount, I do remember being the richest person in the world. I remember the feeling of being wealthy and powerful. I remember all those coins that I saved and how much money I had. I must have been the richest person in the world. And the power that came with it . . . I didn't have to ask my parents if they could buy me candy (they usually said no anyway). I could buy my own candy without asking for money! I was rich and powerful!

Since I was now a business person, at 6 years old, I was always looking for ways to expand my company. I then read somewhere about compound interest. I couldn't believe my eyes! This was free money! All you had to do was put your money in a bank and depending on the interest rate, they would just give you money every month, for free! I sure loved being in Canada, there was money everywhere! Now, the bank just gives you more free money!

The compound interest chart shows how if you invest $10 now and leave it in the bank for a certain amount of time at a certain interest rate, one day you would have $100. Oh my goodness, $100, can you imagine? I did not know anyone with that much money. Since I had no concept of interest rates, that part didn't deter me from anything. I had $10 and I wanted $100. According to this compound interest chart, it was possible. Since I made a couple of dollars a week with bottles, imagine how much faster I could reach $100 if I only invested all the money I made? I was no longer interested in candy. Why would anyone want candy when they could have this much money?

I spoke with my parents about getting a bank account. We ended up at a Royal Bank to open up a savings account. I even had a little book that kept track of all the deposits and any "interest" that they would give me. I had to see this free money thing for myself as I couldn't believe they just give you money.

Again, I had no idea how much I received on my first interest payment, probably something like $0.01 or

$0.02 cents but I do remember seeing that on my little bank book. They actually gave me free money! I could not believe this! They were giving free money! I would stare at this book for hours in amazement. They gave me money for free. I would then try to figure out how much money I would have if I put in another $10. This was so much fun. Any temptation of purchasing anything was gone. I was so amazed by the free money laying on the streets and the free money that banks were giving away that all I wanted to do was put everything I had into the bank and look at my little bank deposit book.

We finally moved from Edmonton to Tumbler Ridge, BC. It's a small mining town when there is something to mine, otherwise a ghost town when there is nothing to mine. My entrepreneurship continued with getting a paper route. I do remember getting paid $0.10 for every paper I delivered. I tried to get as many paper routes as I possibly could as I had all the time in the world to deliver the paper after school. My first non-investment was to save up for a Bon Jovi t-shirt, that one with the long white sleeves and the black front and back. Not sure how long it took me to save up but as soon as I had the $10, I ran to buy that shirt. Of course, I wasn't allowed to wear it but I couldn't be stopped from buying it, since it was my very own money. After this major purchase, I was back to saving every last penny I made.

We then moved to Powell River, BC for my dad's work. I needed another job when I was 10 years old so I found a small book somewhere, titled something like, "101 ways to make money from home." Perfect, surely there must be something that a 10 year old can do. I eventually found, "Dog Walking Service. Perfect, I can walk dogs. I quickly made up a price list, $0.50 for a medium dog and $0.75 for a large dog. Off I went, door to door, again without any fear of rejection. Imagine the things we could accomplish if we didn't have any fear of rejection like I did when I was ten, wow!

Most people didn't have dogs and I'm sure some wouldn't trust a strange 10 year old with their dog either. I did come across this one Italian family, who I still remember, the D'Agostinos'. They had this big, beautiful German Shepard that they let me walk. We set up a schedule and I would walk her at the same time every day, for $0.75. I was now a professional! This job was so much fun! I couldn't believe how many fun things there were to do where people actually paid you to do it. I loved working and seeing this dog every day. Of course, the pay was excellent, the most money I was making up until this time. Yes, I saved all of that.

My parents ended up purchasing a pizza and pasta place, called Dallas 2 for 1 Pizza and Pasta. It was a take out or delivery only place and I have to admit the food was great. After several years of eating the same food and I can still say the food was good then it must be good.

I found out later that my sister and I worked for less than minimum wage. At 13 years old, I wasn't too familiar with labor laws and how an employee gets to have a minimum wage. Had I known then, I would have been amazed all over again that we should be getting paid more. I believe all of the other staff was paid minimum wage except for my sister and me. It didn't really matter since I loved the job anyway.

I worked there doing odds and ends until I was able to deliver pizza. This was the dream job for a 16 year old and I couldn't wait to be doing that. Not only do you get paid for wages but people give you "tips", more free money!

My father helped me purchase my first car. Helping means, he negotiated the deal, not that he paid for it nor that he made any financial contributions. I thought I was paying the owner monthly payments directly but in fact, my father paid for the car and the payments I made to the owner, he just gave to my dad. Good 'ol dad. Those life lessons sure made me a more successful person as oppose to if he just bought it for me.

I had my driver's license at 17, instead of 16 like everyone else. I also moved out of the house at 17 and went to live with a boyfriend. After a few months, I suggested that we purchase a house. He had a really good paying job and I worked at my parent's restaurant and still went to high school. We decided to purchase a house and we qualified for $80,000.

We lived on Texada Island at the time and the realtor came over to show us a few houses within our price range. There was only so much to choose from. While waiting for the next ferry back to Powell River, she said we might as well look at another house since we are there and waiting. We went to see this little a frame wooden home listed at $125,000. I immediately fell in love with! I said that this is my dream house and let's put an offer in on that.

We sat in the realtor's office to fill out the paperwork. "How much do you want to offer?" she asks. I was a little unsure of what she meant to offer. I replied with, "well, $80,000!"

"You can't offer $80,000, that's too low."

How can we not offer that? That is what we are qualified for and that is all the money we have. "Sorry, but that is all we have," I explained. Why would she bother showing me a house worth $125,000 when she knows we only have $80,000? We left the offer at $80,000.

Over the next couple of weeks, we were getting phone calls that the owner will take $110,000. I kept explaining that we only have $80,000 and can't offer more. The next call was that she will accept $100,000. That's great, but we still only have $80,000. To make this book shorter, they eventually accepted our offer of $80,000! I couldn't believe this! My dream home for only $80,000! I love real estate now too!

I was hoping that deal could have completed while I was still 17 years old but it happened just after I turned 18. At 18 years old, that's not bad at all to purchase your first house. This was exciting stuff for me. We lived a very happy life, a little home, some cats and I got a new job at the only restaurant on the island, Texada Island Arms. This would mean that there were only four waitresses on the whole island and I could not believe my great fortune, that I got one of those positions! I absolutely loved being a server and working 4 days on and 4 days off. Life was fantastic!

One day at work, the bookkeeper approached us with a savings plan. We were going to take a couple of dollars of our paychecks every two weeks and have it put into an account which would receive interest on the money. We would then receive all of this at the beginning of December to help with Christmas shopping. I immediately thought, to hell with shopping, think of all the money we will get in December!

Most of the staff signed up for $25 or even $50 per check. I think my checks were about or just under $400 per pay period. I signed up for $300 per paycheck. The bookkeeper came back to explain this to me again as clearly I must have misunderstood. I confirmed that I want $300 taken off every check. My plan was to live off any tips I made and put the rest into the bank. My paychecks were always less than $100 but it was enough to purchase groceries and other essentials and still put my measly paychecks into the bank.

Please note that Texada Island is so small, that there is only one grocery store, a small hotel with that one restaurant, a pub and post office. There is nowhere to spend money on, at least nowhere for me to spend money. I later found out that most people on that island were so bored that all there was to do there was go to the pub and drink or do drugs. To me, wasting money on alcohol or drugs was the most incredibly stupid thing anyone could possibly do. I equated smoking or doing drugs with burning money and there would be no way I would ever do anything that stupid. Once that $20 is gone at the bar, it is done forever and you get nothing for it. To me, spending $20 at a bar was a lot until I found out most people spent at least $100. Who could possibly spend $100 on alcohol? That money could have been saved! Not sure if I was naïve or what one would call it but I am thankful every day that I had no interest in drugs or alcohol and was never influenced by that.

I was addicted to watching my money grow. I was excited to go to the bank and deposit money into savings. Once that savings grew to $1,000, I would then convert it into a term deposit that paid even more interest. I was then excited to see how many of these $1,000 term deposits I could get!

Eventually, things didn't work out with the boyfriend and we went our separate ways. He stayed in the house and I moved to the big city with my big $10,000 buy-out from my portion of the house. I invested this money into a 2 bedroom condo in Surrey, BC. I paid around $130,000 and lived there for seven years. Over those years, I rented out the other bedroom as well as the loft to pay for part of my mortgage payments and to pay down the mortgage faster.

After those seven years, I sold that same condo for $230,000. I made the $100,000 on the appreciation of the condo without having to do anything else as well as had an extra $30,000 from paying down that mortgage. So, over seven years, that $10,000 grew to $130,000. I wasn't sure of any other investment that could do that.

I purchased what they call a mega house for about $500,000. It was a two story with a full basement. I lived in the top part of the house and rented out the two basement suites that I had in order to help with the mortgage payments. I also went off to work as a realtor.

As the mortgage on this house decreased and the equity increased due to the boom that Vancouver experienced during those years, the house appreciated to $650,000 in less than two years. I took out a line of credit and used part of that money to purchase another mega mansion for about $600,000. It was the same type of home, two-story with two basement suites. I rented out this house along with the suites and made great cash flow every month.

All was fun and games until I experienced the "tenants" that landlords speak of! These stories are so juicy that I am saving them for the next book. Trust me, I have enough of those stories to full up a whole new book. At the end of the day, these same tenants are the reason why I will be sitting on a beach in a few years, sipping my Pina Colada while they are still renting. Sometimes, it is worth it!

I ended up purchasing another condo in Richmond, BC to move out of Surrey. I lived there for a couple of months until the condo flooded and I had to move out.

While standing there with my feet in sewage water, I was incredibly calm. I knew that for some reason, this was an opportunity in disguise and that I would appreciate it someday. It's very odd how sometimes we just know these things.

I ended up not wanting to move back in there after the flood. With all the furniture and items still there, I thought I would try to rent it out furnished. I received a really good response and some pretty good money for it as well. I figured that I would leave it as a furnished rental and rent myself a brand new penthouse suite along with all new furniture.

As I sat in my penthouse, I dabbled with the idea of renting that suite out as well. I wonder how much I could rent it for. It turned out, that someone wanted to rent it furnished for $3,000 per month. I was only paying $1,600 in rent, so this would be a huge profit of $1,400 per month! I ended up grabbing my bags and moving out, leaving that as a furnished rental as well.

After a while, I had some clients ask me to rent their suites as well. Those suites did so well, that their friends and families gave me their suites to rent also. And, as they say, "The rest is history!"

Remember how there was the big controversy about the 99% or the 1%? Well, allow me to weigh on that. As you progress from the 99% up to the 1%, you will understand where everyone comes from!

That was a fun time and boy did I ever make many friends during that time. At least I cleaned out my useless friends from Facebook after that fiasco. Let me lose a couple more readers here as well with my famous two cents worth.

My first thoughts were why do we even have these two groups? I thought we were all Canadians or Americans, we all eat at McDonalds, we all went to high school, we all laugh and cry and so forth. Now it seems that we need to separate each other into two groups and yell at each other and make fun of the other group. That makes sense to me, a great way to pull this country together!

Although I will admit that I do not know the entire story about what was happening nor am I interested in brushing up on that part of the news, I do have a general idea. I prefer to hear people's opinions directly from individuals themselves and engage in those discussions. I would rather not read about opinions in the newspapers as they are not always accurate and people's words are misconstrued at times. I prefer not to form an opinion about an individual that I have never met, no matter what I have read about them. Yes, for some people it's difficult not to have an opinion about, such as Hitler or others like him. Those people have so much evidence against them that I have convinced myself that they are bad people.

We then have celebrities and other famous people that we all have a strong opinion of. I like Oprah Winfrey because she seems to be a powerful woman, she seems to do a lot of charitable work and I have seen through television the smiles on people's faces that are a result of her actions. I could be wrong, perhaps it's not even her money that she is giving away, perhaps those ideas aren't even hers to feed hungry children, perhaps she is just doing it all for the cameras and her ratings. I don't know because I have never met her. People's behaviors on television might annoy me but I can't say that I don't like someone if I have never met them.

I get very amused when I hear people talk about someone in a negative way when they have never even met them. I jump right in to say, "Wow, you have met her? Is she really a bitch?" Then I always get the obvious look like, "Of course not!"

So I persist, "Oh," sounding quite surprised, "Then how do you know she's a bitch?"

"Well, I read about her in a magazine!" is the obvious answer. Of course, you read about her in a magazine . . . so it must be true! Okay, so now the entire world will also think that she is a bitch because she has now been exposed in a magazine and now everyone knows. Please, a lot of those magazines do not report the truth. Gossip magazines have contracts with talent agents so that they have access to stories and photos and have something to write. Even if their agents submit a story, it still does not make it true. It amazes me how many people believe everything they read! But that's fine, the magazine industry loves people like that who continue to purchase magazines because they believe everything they read.

Is the National Inquirer still around? That's a magazine, so anything they write must be true, right? A woman gave birth to a baby elephant ... must be true right? It's in a magazine. The UFO landed in someone's backyard ... must be true! It's in a magazine! People that believe everything they read sure have small brains and have none of their own thoughts to actually think about what they read to analyze it. Then again, I took a course at University that taught us not to believe everything we read, so maybe it's not common knowledge after all.

Now we get into the more serious stuff: the crooks! Those people on Wall Street that "stole" our money! Yes, they have been making a master plan for 150 years so that in 2008 they can steal everything all at once! Again, "Wow, you met that guy and he stole your money?"

"Well, no I never met him but he stole my money! It was written in the paper!" Then is must be true, right?

Years ago, during the dot com boom, I used to save all of my money. My roommate at the time gave me a hot stock tip: Nortel is going to go up! Well, if he said it then it must be true. I quickly invested about $3,000 and sat by and couldn't wait for it to go up. What ended up happening was quite the contrary, it went down. As a matter of fact, it went down so far that it went out of town! Gone, just like that. All $3,000 of my money just vanished. So now it's time for the blame game: who stole my money? It's certainly not me because I am a hardworking, innocent investor. I am a single mother who needed that money. Who stole my money?

Let's have closer look at this little scenario. The "hot stock tip" came from my roommate, who was a telephone technician for a local phone company. Divorced with two kids, he lived with a roommate because he couldn't afford to live on his own. He had no savings and lived paycheck to paycheck. But he had a "hot stock tip". If this tip was so hot, why did he not purchase any stock for himself? Hmmm, that makes me wonder. I mean, it was guaranteed to go up, he told me so!

I guess I can also call up Nortel and tell them that I am a hardworking, single mother who invested several months' worth of my paychecks into their company. I couldn't afford to lose that. They stole it from me and I want it back!

Honestly, perhaps I was an idiot. Anyone that just takes a hot stock tip and goes with it without checking it out is an idiot. Looking back on that now, that was just plain stupid. I really had no one to blame but myself.

Even when you hire a professional, do you check their background at all? How do you know that they are qualified? Just because they work at an office and claim to have a title, does not automatically make them knowledgeable. When you first start to invest your money, you are required to sign some papers. Those papers clearly say that they are not responsible for any financial losses. You are paying for their "advice" but it is up to you to take the advice. At no time is it their fault if you make or lose money. Therefore, anyone that invests in any investment bank, stocks or with other financial planners, you are still responsible for those decisions, period!

This country (both Canada and the United States) does not reward anyone for their hard work. What is wrong with making millions of dollars? Why can we not be happy for those people? I am constantly hearing these super rich people or CEO's get criticized for making a ton of money. Why should they not? Is there something wrong with that? If so, perhaps point me to some graph where it says what is acceptable to make? I certainly wouldn't want to make too much money and be bad mouthed because I make too much.

Is one million per month too much money? So if I am offered that amount at a company, what do I say? Do I decline and say, "Oh sorry, that is just way too much money and not very fair to all of the other people that don't make this much." How about this: let me know if this is acceptable, "Wow, one million per month, I better give half of my paycheck to charity every single month because one million is way too much for one person." If you are complaining that someone is making too much money, why don't you make a little graph or a scale so that the rest of us, who work hard to make that goal, will know what is the most we can make. This way, I can look at your stupid chart and go back and let them know what an acceptable amount every month would be in order not to offend the rest of the Joe Schmoes!

If that is the way you think, you would be better off living in a communist country. This way, every citizen can make the exactly the same amount of money, no matter what. You don't need to worry about savings because you can't have any so you have to spend every check. You don't need to look at your lazy neighbor that does nothing, because, don't worry he gets the same paycheck as you. You went to college? Who cares, you can get the same paycheck. You will just be a doctor instead of a waitress, but you love the job and in the end, so do the waitress, so everyone gets the same paycheck. There you go, that is the place for you.

Your worries will now be over. Your neighbor won't work on the weekends to write that top selling book because why bother, he won't be able to keep more money than you anyways. No need to invent anything because the government will own it, not you. Sounds fair, right? Everyone can drive the same cars and all houses will be relatively the same. There will no longer be any gaps between the rich and the poor as we will all be the same. That is more up your alley, isn't it? Now we can all be fair!

Do you team players on team 99 have any concept of what team 1 goes through to get to where they are? I heard this guy complaining while sitting on the couch, smoking a joint and drinking a beer, unemployed, without an education and no ambition, bad mouthing the team 1%. He said he wants to smash all the faces of team 1%. Why? Who did he meet personally to even know anyone from team 1? What does he know about them? He wants to smash all of their faces? Well, the couch that he sits on was from a company owned by someone on team 1. So was his cell phone that he was using and the iPhone. Bad-mouthing on Facebook, are we? Well, hate to break it to you, but yes, team 1. Did that guy who invented Facebook steal? Haha, don't answer that one; it's a joke!

The point is, the lifestyle we all enjoy, good and bad, is all because of these ambitious team 1% people. Everyone sure did encourage them to work really hard and get rich. However, once they achieved that goal, those same people now bad-mouth them because they are too rich. They all had a dream and a vision. Some came by it by luck; others were inherited. Either way, these people should be celebrated, not blamed.

Henry Ford, yes, he deserves to make billions of dollars. Sam Walton, yes, he does deserve billions. He gave it all to his family, and yes, they all deserve that too. It's his family! Who says you have to give to charity or give it all away? What the hell for? Then there is Warren Buffett, one of the richest men in the world. He isn't leaving too much to his kids. He'd rather give it all away. That is fine also but certainly does not make one person better than the other.

So often I hear people saying, "But I work hard." So? So do a lot of people. All those people that worked at the factory at Ford, sweating all day long and getting dirty, working long hours, yes, they worked hard. Yes, Henry Ford was probably up in an office somewhere in a suit, sitting and maybe even playing poker at a table. Should Mr. Ford come down and say, "Son, today you physically worked harder than me. You should take more money than me today." That would be the most retarded thing I ever heard!

Those team 1% people make it for reasons that team 99 would never understand. Take my good couch-sitting friend. I asked him why he isn't working and he tells me there are no jobs. No jobs? None at all? Every single job in Canada has been taken and there are no jobs left.

I continued on, "Have you been looking?"

"No, I just know there are no jobs out there," he answers. How the hell does he know? Did the television report that? Was there breaking news about, don't bother looking for jobs. There are none left. We will advise you when there are some so that you can get up off the couch and go and get one. Or did the guy who brought him his weed tell him that? Sorry, but even the guy who brought the weed has a job! Not that I am encouraging becoming a drug dealer, just making a silly point.

Do jobs show up at your doorstep? Does one just wait for someone to knock at your door and tell you that you have a job? Or does the phone ring? Maybe if you check your Facebook, they will message you with a, "We have a job for you". I don't know, I haven't looked for a job in years. I do remember though, when I did work for someone else, I called them! I was more of a pest by calling all the time about work than waiting for someone to call me.

I know a lot of people put their life savings into these big companies that failed. I also know that those CEOs of that company made tens of millions of dollars in bonuses. It is a free country, and everyone is free to invest wherever they want. There are thousands of companies to invest in and different investment vehicles, such as real estate. No one was forced to invest in certain companies just like everyone was free to verify their information and make their own decisions on where to invest. What really picks my nose is, no one complained while everyone was making money, and everyone thought they were so smart because they picked a stock or a company that had good returns. As soon as those same investments weren't making any money, or worse, disappeared, all of a sudden everyone is a victim. Everyone suddenly has a story, and everyone has been robbed. It's no longer their fault; now it's someone else's fault.

They read the headlines about a CEO getting a 25 million dollar bonus. First, it must be true because everything written in a newspaper is true, and second, they probably received it all in a bag of cash too, right? Is it possible that their bonus was by way of stock? Is it possible that when everyone else lost their stocks, the CEOs also lost their bonus at the same time? Even if they received their big bonuses in cash delivered to their door, so what? You still made the decision to invest in a particular company. All that information is public information and wasn't hidden from anyone. Anyone could have read about that before they invested their money or their life savings. How many people actually did though? If you can't be bothered to do your own research and make your own choices, then why blame others when the going gets tough?

Yes, of course, I feel horrible that people lost their life savings. Just like I feel horrible for those CEOs who worked extremely hard all their lives building a billion dollar conglomerate, just to lose it all overnight. Why are these people made out like they have no feelings towards the situation whatsoever? It's not a non-profit investment company and the more money they make for the company and, in turn, the shareholders, the more they should be entitled to when its bonus time. I have absolutely no problem with their bonuses or the size of them. As a matter of fact, I hope that one day it can be me getting that big of a bonus. Why the hell not?

CHAPTER 10

Contract, Manuals & Checklists

The following contracts may be used and tailored to your specific company or property. You may also purchase these for your use on our website for a nominal fee. These are suggested contracts, manuals, and checklists. Even if you just hire a housekeeper for your own home, the checklist included here is a perfect list to give to your housekeeper!

Independent Contractor

Housekeeping/Guest Services

1. This contract is made between (contractor name,) hereby known as the "contractor" of (contractor address) and (your company name), hereby known as the "company". The current phone number for the contractor is (phone number). If any changes of the above information occur, the contractor

will immediately advise the "company" in writing.

2. The contractor acknowledges that they are an independent contractor and not an employee of (your company). The contractor is responsible for filing their own taxes, their own expenses, and paying any other government fees. The "company" will be paying the contractor a set rate per service with no further compensation now or in the future.

3. This contract consists of three parts: Independent Contractor: Housekeeping/ Guest Services; Housekeeping Manual, and Guest Representative Manual.

4. The following are the current rates for services payable to housekeepers and guest representatives:

One-bedroom suites: $xx
Two-bedroom suites: $xx
Three-bedroom suites: $xx
Gas expense per suite: $x
Extra cleans: as agreed upon through email
Check-in fee: $xx
Shopping fee: $xx
Other fees: as agreed upon per company emails

There will be no further compensation other than the above mentioned rates. For other rates, please email the "company" directly for confirmation as they are based on an individual basis.

5. The housekeeping portion of the job is detailed in the separate document, entitled, "housekeeping manual." It is attached and forms a part of this contract. The job description must be followed in detail. Each rate is based on completing the entire job description, and failing to complete the entire job description may result in deductions to the above mentioned rates.

6. Any guests who complain about the cleanliness of their suites, the contractor is expected and required to go back and tend to all deficiencies of that suite within 24 hours. If the independent contractor is not available for a re-clean, they may ask another housekeeper to re-clean on their behalf. Compensation may either be made between the two contractors as financial or as an exchange for a future re-clean. In the event of a dispute over compensation, the "company" will make the final decision between the two contractors.

7. In the event that the suite had an excessive amount of deficiencies, the "company" may cancel the fee completely as the guests will need to be refunded for their cleaning fee. Although the guest contracts specify that there are no refunds on the cleaning fee, if there are special circumstances, such as an excessive amount of deficiencies, the housekeeper will forfeit their cleaning fee.

8. The guest representative portion of this contract is detailed in a separate document, entitled, "Guest Representative Manual." It is attached and forms a part of this contract. The job description must be followed in detail. Each rate is based on completing the entire job description, and failing to complete the entire job description may result in deductions to the above-mentioned rates.

9. Current rates for check-in are $xx per check-in. This fee consists of meeting the guest with keys, completing a check-in form, and completing a pre-authorization. Failing to complete any of the three steps will result in a deduction in the check-in fee.

10. Privacy and Confidentiality: All guest information such as phone numbers, email addresses, home addresses, names, or any other personal information about the guest is strictly the property of the "company". No contractor at any time will possess any of this information on their personal phones or emails or any other device or notebook. At no time ever will a contractor contact the guests directly from their personal phone or their personal email. Contact with guests can only be made from company cell phones and company emails. Each and every occurrence, meaning every call and every email, will result in a $50 fine. There are absolutely no exceptions to this rule.

B. All owner information is strictly the property of the "company". No contractor at any time will possess any of this information on their personal phones or emails. At no time ever will a contractor contact the owners directly from their personal phone or their personal emails. At no time will the contractor provide an owner with their personal information, such as phone number, email address, or home address. Contact with owners can only be made from company cell phones and company emails. Each and every occurrence, meaning every call and every email, will result in a $50 fine. There are absolutely no exceptions to this rule.

C. All information, contracts, documents, policies, manuals, rules, or the like are the private and confidential information of the "company". No part of this information may be copied, distributed, used, or borrowed in any way whatsoever for any purposes. Any breach of the privacy and confidentiality policies may result in termination of the Independent Contractor contract, and further legal action may result.

D. The only emails that may be distributed to the guests, owners, potential owners, or potential guests are the following:

Phone Number: (your company phone number)
Email Address: (your company email addresses)

E. Contractor information may never be distributed to any individual without the prior written consent of the contractor themselves. This includes any requests for personal information about or for the owner of the company. Any requests to speak with a manager must be directed to the supervisor and can be reached at (your company phone number). This is the only manager or owner information that may be given to anyone requesting this information. A breach of this rule will result in fines from $50 and up.

11. Termination: Any contractor wishing to terminate their contract must provide at least two weeks' written notice. Failure to provide a two weeks' notice may result in the contractor forfeiting any compensation already owed to the contractor. All property of the "company" must be returned to the company prior to receiving final pay. The two weeks' notice may be shortened if agreed to in writing by both parties.

B. The "company" may terminate the contract of any contractor with less than two weeks' notice for cause or for a breach or constant breaching of any of the rules or policies. Already-owed fees to the contractor will still be payable upon returning all of the company property, minus any fines or fees payable to the company.

12. Changes to Contract: Any changes or updates to this contract will be made in writing via email and sent out to the contractors. A response will be required through email acknowledging receiving the updates and will form a part of this contract.

13. Assignments: Each contractor will be assigned their own individual days. You are contracted and responsible for the particular day that you are hired for. Any changes, days off, time off, etc., is the responsibility of each individual contractor to find their own replacement for the contracted days. The "company" will not be responsible for finding a replacement for the contractor days. The "company" must be advised immediately if there will be another individual working on the contractor's day.

B. Each contractor is required to be available for the entire day of their contracted day and must be available to answer calls and/or emails within 15 minutes. The contractor is expected to answer the company phone when it rings and not let it go to voicemail. Should it go to voicemail, the contractor is expected to return all calls within 15 minutes. It is recommended not to schedule other appointments or make other plans for contracted days. If necessary, please advise the office of your plans so that everyone is aware of your whereabouts. Failing to return calls or answer calls is considered late or absent, and the contractor will be fined accordingly, starting at $25 and up.

Housekeeping Manual

The following information is provided for you in order to make sure that every item on this list is complete. Any items that are missing/incomplete, you will not be paid for as it will be considered incomplete or will need to be redone. Regular inspections of suites will be conducted periodically, and progress reports may be emailed to you. You will be expected to correct any work where guests have called in to complain.

We cannot have any customer complaints when it comes to the cleanliness of suites. This checklist should eliminate customer complaints or at least lower them. Let's strive to satisfy the OCD guests so they don't go elsewhere because once our guests leave and don't come back, the other company becomes successful and we become unemployed. We rely on every guest to pay our bills.

There is no reason why we should not satisfy the most detail-oriented or hard-to-please guest. This is what should make us stand out from the crowd.

Checklist before leaving office:

— Key to suite/suites needing service
— Info of suite (i.e., parking space #, suite #)
— Proper amount of clean linens—sheets, duvet covers, towels, bathmats, dish towels
— Cleaning supplies: clean and dry rags, all-purpose cleaner in spray bottles, toilet paper, garbage bags, mop, magic eraser.
— Check to make sure you have ALL of the linens necessary. Never rely on someone else's word that it's all there. Please double check for yourself.
— Check to see if the next guest checking in needs an extra cot—along with it, they will need an extra towel set and sheets for the cot—don't forget the pillow! Confirm if guests have any other requests for their suites.

Make sure you knock before entering the suite as the guests may still be inside.

Should a guest still be in the suite, you are not allowed to enter the suite to start cleaning. Let the guests know that you will return. You must call the office immediately to advise that the guests have not checked out yet. The office will call the guests to make arrangements. Even if the guests grant you permission to come in and start cleaning, you may never enter a suite until a guest has left. This ensures that housekeeping is not being accused of stealing any items that the guests may have lost or misplaced. You may not leave the linens inside as the guests sometimes need an extra towel and will take from the new, clean linen. Failure to comply with these basic rules may result in not getting paid for the suite.

***When you first enter the suite, please follow procedure in the following order:

1. Make sure that the fobs/garage door openers are on the kitchen table. The spare key should have been left under the front door. Put the key that you found on the floor in front of the door and attach it to the keychain with the garage door opener that should be on the kitchen table. DO NOT attach it to the keys that you were given to access the suite. You must call the office immediately if the keys are not left in the suite.

2. Check for any damage to or missing items from the suite. You must call the office immediately if there is any damage or missing items.

3. Count all of the towels and make sure they are all there. Check for any damages, stains to the towels. Should any towels be damaged, stained, or missing, you must call the office to report it. Every bathroom has two large, two medium, and two small. They are also called two large bath towels, two medium hand towels, and two facecloths. There is also one bathmat per bathroom. This is for every bathroom. Take note of any damages, stains, or missing towels.

4. Check to make sure that all the lights are working. Turn on all of the lights to make sure they all work. Change any and all light bulbs that are not working. The basic light bulbs should be left in the housekeeping car at all times. Light bulbs specific to a suite should be purchased at least three at a time. Change the light bulbs and leave one underneath the sink for future use.

5. Laundry:
Remove all dirty laundry from beds, bathrooms, and kitchen. Double check for stains and make a note to advise the Laundromat there are stains so they can ensure they are removed. Upon receiving the laundry back from the Laundromat, double check to ensure that the stain has been removed. If it has not, remove the item from the laundry bag and replace it with a clean, non-stained item. Report this item to guest services so the guest can be billed accordingly.

*Do not use any towels with any stains on them.

If possible, laundry can be done in the suite while cleaning. Put similar colors into the machine on a "quick wash". Use hot water and detergent for sterilization. As soon as a wash is done, put into the dryer. This should not take more than 25 minutes for wash and 40 minutes for dry (depending on dryer).

Make sure to clean out the lint trap in the dryer and wipe down the washing machine if dirty.

Bathrooms:

- ✓ Including sinks, tubs, showers, toilets (also behind toilets) mirrors, floors, and walls
- ✓ Disinfect all fixtures and surfaces. All surfaces should be shining. Take extra care to ensure there is no dirt around the silver rink in the sink or around the faucets. There should not be any dirt and it should look like a brand new sink.
- ✓ Double check to ensure there are no hairs or cloth remnants in the sinks, tubs, toilets, or other surfaces.
- ✓ Empty trash receptacles and wipe down inside and outside of can if needed. Leave an extra garbage bag inside the trash bin for future use for the guests.
- ✓ Check the mirrors within a half hour AFTER cleaning them to ensure they have dried properly and there are no streak marks or any remnants from cleaning cloths.
- ✓ Clean towels put into bathrooms—one set per person. Extra set put under sink if no room on racks. (1 x large bath towel, 1 x hand towel, 1 x wash cloth). Extra towels can also be displayed on top of the toilet (bowl, not lid), on top of the counter, or even on the bed. Ensure that the towels are folded perfectly, all corners match, and that they are evenly placed.
- ✓ Clean underneath the sink and ensure that there are no hairs, dirt, or anything else left behind underneath the sink.

- ✓ Wipe the inside of the cupboard doors underneath the sink.
- ✓ Please two extra rolls of toilet paper closest to the toilet.
- ✓ There should also be a hair dryer underneath the sink. Please report if this is missing.
- ✓ Don't forget bathmats (1 x per bathroom). Ensure that this is folded, all corners together, and that it does not look sloppy, dirty, or stained.
- ✓ Toilet paper on roll should be at least 50% full, otherwise, replace with brand new roll of toilet paper. Return any unused toilet paper to office.
- ✓ Place "condiments" on sink—(1 x body gel, 1 x shampoo, 1 x conditioner, 1 x lotion, 1 x shower cap, 1 x mouthwash, 1 x bar soap).
- ✓ Body gel should be placed near the shower. The shower cap should be placed away from the sink or the shower so that it does not get wet.
- ✓ Towels hung on towel racks should be folded perfectly, straight edges and all corners together. There should be one bath towel and one hand towel hung on the towel rack. The rest of the towels should be underneath the sink, not in the drawer.
- ✓ Double check to ensure the sinks and tub drain easily, by themselves. This should be reported by housekeeping, not guests. Always have a spare drain remover in the car and pour into clogs. This should be done at the beginning of a clean to allow ample

time to declog and then flush out with hot running water. There is also an odour to this product so ensure that the fans are on and the odour is eliminated before leaving.

✓ Ensure that the shower walls are clean, the bottom of the tub, and that there is no lime residue around the bathtub drain. Use CLR to remove any traces of this.

✓ Ensure that the walls of the shower and tubs are dry and shiny.

✓ Wipe down all of the walls and double check that there are no marks or stains on the walls. Use a magic erasure to clean off any marks and rewipe the walls with a wet cloth. Any marks that do not come off should be reported and photographed.

✓ Ensure that everything is working, faucets, drains, toilet, showers, towel racks are not loose, cupboards are not loose, all lights work, the fan turns on and off. Report any maintenance issues immediately. **Light bulbs are not to be reported to maintenance but changed by housekeeping.

✓ Floors should always be washed and dried and no one should enter the bathrooms after the floors are clean. Never wear shoes or bare feet on clean floors but wear socks on the floors instead.

Beds:

✓ Each bed should have:
✓ One fitted sheet

✓ Either a duvet cover or two flat sheets
✓ Duvet
✓ 4 pillows per bed for a king, queen, and double. Twin beds should have one pillow.
✓ Decorative pillow
✓ Double check to ensure that no sheets have stains or are discoloured.
✓ Double check to ensure that there is no hair left behind, anywhere!
✓ Make sure that the beds look fluffy, pillows are straight, and nothing hanging off.
✓ Pillow covers need to match.
✓ Triple check underneath the bed. It also needs to be vacuumed and clean.
✓ Shake the bed and check to ensure that there are no broken or damaged parts of the bed. We MUST ensure that the beds are safe before a guest lies on the bed. As this is a safety issue, failure to ensure a bed is not broken may result in not getting paid for a suite.
✓ **If you feel that any of the linens, duvets, pillows, or beds are not up to an OCD guest's standards, please discuss with supervisor.

Bedrooms

✓ Check underneath the beds and ensure there are no forgotten items or garbage. Vacuum underneath the bed.
✓ Wipe down all the walls and use magic erasure to remove ALL scuff marks.

✓ Look into the closet and remove all excess items and garbage. Remove all scuff marks and wipe down walls.

✓ There should be no dust inside the closet, along the baseboard.

✓ If there are extra pillows, they should be on top of the closet, with a pillow case on the pillow.

✓ Check to make sure the lights are working, windows open, and all side tables are wiped down.

✓ Wipe all baseboards from dust.

✓ Wipe the light bulb inside the lamp.

Kitchen

✓ Disinfect all fixtures and surfaces.

✓ Open all cupboards and drawers—check for crumbs or disorganization.

✓ Make sure that there is NO FOOD in cupboards or fridge/freezer.

✓ Wipe down inside of fridge and freezer.

✓ Clean out dishwasher, put dry dishes away.

✓ Take inventory of how many dishes/glassware are remaining.

✓ Empty garbage receptacles, spot clean and replace bag—put an extra bag under sink.

✓ Wipe down cupboards, walls, appliances.

✓ Check to see if the stove or microwave needs a clean inside.

✓ Place clean dish towels neatly on counter or oven handrail.

✓ Wipe down all appliances on the outside.

✓ Leave the following items neatly displayed near the coffee maker: regular coffee, decaf coffee, tea, and sugar/whitener.

Living Room

Check for the following appliances to ensure they work:

✓ Suite phone, call yourself to ensure you can make outgoing calls. Call the suite to ensure that the ringer is turned on and the phone rings.
✓ Ensure that the suite information book is correct by verifying that the number is correct.
✓ Turn the television on and off to ensure the remote and TV are working.
✓ Have a look at the Internet modem to ensure all the lights are on.
✓ Check all of the lamps by turning them on and off.
✓ Make sure the heat is turned completely off during the summer.
✓ During the colder months, ensure the heat is turned to 15.
✓ Turn the microwave on and off.
✓ Turn on all of the elements on the stove to ensure they all work.
✓ The oven should be working as well. Needs to be self-cleaned every once in a while.
✓ Turn on all the taps to ensure they work.

✓ Check to make sure all the drains are draining easily.

✓ Run a pot of hot water through the coffee pot to ensure that it works and to clean the system.

✓ Test the toaster and hot water kettle/electric kettle.

✓ Ensure the appliances don't have any missing or broken parts and report to supervisor if necessary.

✓ Check all garage door openers to ensure that they work.

✓ Check doors to ensure they all lock and unlock easily.

✓ Check to make sure that the vacuum works (you would know this by using it).

✓ Double-check the inventory sheet to ensure all items are left inside the condo.

✓ Washer and dryer should both be working.

✓ Open and close all the windows and doors to make sure they work.

✓ Fans should be working, turn them all on and off.

Housekeeping Checklist

Before you leave for the suite make sure you have the following:

✓ Keys to the correct suite

✓ Info for the suite (parking number, suite address, and number)

✓ Check your linens to make sure you are bringing the right amount. Confirm the amount and sizes of beds and ensure there are enough linens for all beds. All beds must be made at all times.

✓ Cleaning supplies in the black backpack (make sure you fill up the bottles)

✓ Check the notes for the next check-in of that suite to see if the guest needs anything extra, like a cot or playpen.

✓ Ensure that you have extra light bulbs.

When arriving at the suite:

✓ Knock to make sure guest is not in the suite before you walk in.

✓ Make sure there is a key left under the door and attach it to the keychain they left on the table right away. Put the keys you got in the suite in a separate area. You must call immediately if the keys are not left in the suite.

✓ Check for any damage to or missing items from the suite, and email or call the reservations department if anything is damaged or missing.

✓ There is an inventory checklist at the back of the guest information book. Please go over the list to confirm that everything is there. Any missing items must be reported to the office right away.

Bedroom

- ✓ Strip the beds.
- ✓ Count bed linens, make sure all linens are there, look for stains—take pictures if stained.
- ✓ Make bed, look for hair or lint.
- ✓ 4 pillows on all beds, except twins or cots which have 2 pillows
- ✓ Clean any mirrors in room, make sure there are no streaks or smudges and, of course, no fingerprints.
- ✓ Dust pictures, tables, dressers, lamps.
- ✓ Wipe down baseboards with Simple Green.
- ✓ Wipe window ledges.
- ✓ Magic erase any marks on walls.
- ✓ Vacuum or swiffer under all beds and look for anything left under the bed.
- ✓ Wipe inside any drawers and check for any items left.
- ✓ Clean and check inside closet for anything left by guest. All hangers must match and be presentable.
- ✓ Clean light switches.
- ✓ Wipe light bulb inside of any lamps.
- ✓ Make sure all lights work.
- ✓ Wipe windows and check for any fingerprints.
- ✓ Check and confirm that the alarm clocks are not set.
- ✓ Vacuum or swiffer or sweep and mop floors. No footprints are to be left.

Bathroom

- ✓ Clean sink, run the water to make sure sink is draining properly. If not, clean the drain.
- ✓ Clean tub inside and out and the shower walls. Shine faucets.
- ✓ Run the water in the tub to see if draining properly. If not, clean the drain.
- ✓ Clean shower grouts if dirty.
- ✓ Clean shower glass doors if they have glass doors, inside with bathroom cleaner, outside with Windex.
- ✓ Clean inside toilet and outside of toilet bowl.
- ✓ Clean behind toilet bowl and floor behind toilet by hand.
- ✓ Clean bathroom mirror—no streaks or smudges.
- ✓ Check shower curtain—no mold or mildew allowed. If so, shower liner must be changed immediately.
- ✓ Magic erase any marks on walls.
- ✓ Clean light switches and make sure all lights are working.
- ✓ Clean the baseboards; do not just dust them.
- ✓ Clean the garbage bin if dirty; if not, just give it a wipe. Leave an extra garbage bag inside.
- ✓ Clean the floor by hand. Vacuum first!
- ✓ Clean bathroom fans when needed.

✓ 2 sets of towels are to be left in each bathroom. 2 large, 2 hand, and 2 face. All towels must match.

✓ 1 soap, 1 shampoo, 1 conditioner, 1 body wash are to be left for guests per bathroom.

✓ Leave one extra roll of toilet paper inside bathroom cabinet closest to toilet.

✓ Extra bed or cot is to get their own set of towels and amenities.

✓ Hairdryer should be in the master bathroom under the sink.

✓ Cleaning also means sanitizing.

Kitchen

✓ Get rid of any open items left by guests, anything that is not on our inventory list.

✓ Clean outside of dishwasher, and make sure inside is clean.

✓ Check dishwasher for any dishes, or do dishes if left by guest. Report to the reservations department if all dishes have been left for us to clean.

✓ Clean microwave in and out.

✓ Clean fridge inside; wash out fridge drawers.

✓ Clean outside of fridge with stainless steel cleaner—no smudges, streaks, or fingerprints. If wood door fridge, wipe down with Simple Green.

✓ Clean stovetop to shine. Use glass-top stove cleaner and scrubber when necessary.

✓ Clean the back of the stovetop to get rid of any grease splatters.

✓ Wipe inside of oven to get crumbs out. Self-clean will be done on special cleans.

✓ Wipe down all appliances, including crumbs in toaster.

✓ Check to make sure garborator works. If not, report to office immediately.

✓ Leave coffee and tea and sugar, etc. by the coffee pot, nicely displayed.

✓ Quickly wipe out drawers and cupboards.

✓ Make sure plates, glasses, cups, and pots are organized in cupboards and drawers to resemble store displays.

✓ Clean under sink and inside of doors.

✓ Clean sink and shine faucets.

✓ Clean kitchen counter.

✓ Clean all the kitchen cupboard doors on outside and inside if dirty.

✓ Wipe garbage can.

✓ Clean floor by hand. Vacuum or sweep first.

✓ Throw out any chipped or broken glasses or dishes. Report to reservations department and replace that day.

✓ Clean dining room tables. If glass, wipe the top and underneath with Windex or glass cleaner.

✓ Check that all lights work and all appliances work.

✓ Leave one dish towel on oven handle.

✓ Under sink place the following: new garbage bag on garbage bin, extra large black garbage bag, 2 dishwasher tabs, dish rags.

Living room

✓ Dust all appliances, tables, artwork and lamps.
✓ Clean window ledges.
✓ Clean inside of windows when any marks appear, including fingerprints.
✓ Clean balcony doors, no fingerprints.
✓ Check that all lights work and the TV and remotes work.
✓ Wipe down couches. Take out the cushions if they come out, clean any crumbs, etc.
✓ Move the couch and sweep and mop under it.
✓ Clean baseboards.
✓ Vacuum floors and mop. No footprints are to be seen.

Notes

✓ No items are to be left in suite, other than what is on inventory list, or what guest has requested.
✓ Remember to call or email the reservations department immediately if something is damaged or missing.
✓ If there is excessive garbage left in the suite, email the reservations department to report this.

- ✓ If there are any stains on carpets, use carpet cleaner and remove right away!! Email with pictures to the reservations department.
- ✓ Wash the inside of fans if dusty and dirty.
- ✓ Quickly check inventory list when in each room. If missing anything, please contact the reservations department right away.
- ✓ Report any maintenance issues to office immediately and also inform Housekeeping Manager.
- ✓ Place all linens, towels, etc., into the laundry bag and label it with the suite number. DO NOT place dirty cloths into the same bag as it stains the rest of the linens.
- ✓ Use suite phone to call once done to ensure that the suite phone works and so that the office is aware that the suite is ready.
- ✓ Clean the lint from the dryer if there is any there.
- ✓ Any complaints from guests regarding cleans, you will be expected to go back and re-clean or resolve any issues that the guest had. A dirty suite ruins a guest's experience, and even though you may go back to re-clean, the damage has already been done. In order to cut down on having to go back, please follow this checklist and double check the suite before leaving.

New Listing Checklist

Property_____

- ✓ Book Photographer: Have the name of a photographer on hand for last-minute bookings.
- ✓ Request MLS listing for information from your local realtor. These sheets have a lot of information about your property.
- ✓ Make a write-up for property.
- ✓ Choose the best photos, at least 12, and submit to the marketing department or the person in charge of your website.
- ✓ Make a guest information package. Include all local information and closest grocery stores, banks, points of interest, and any other information that a guest will require.
- ✓ Please check off each item on this sheet as it is completed.
- ✓ Please add the date of completion after each item.
- ✓ Email all information to your reservations department or upload to reservations system.
- ✓ Have the suite information completely filled out by the owner, and email to the reservation department. If you are doing your own, have all of this information ready on one sheet.
- ✓ Get a void check from the owner for payment and email to the accounting department.

If you are doing your own, have your
accounting and payment systems ready.

✓ Get at least three sets of keys from owner.
They must be signed for. If you are doing
your own, have at least three sets ready.
You must keep one set for yourself at all
times, and never give all of your keys to the
guests and have nothing left for yourself. I
know that sometimes the guests are so nice
and trustworthy, but you must always have
one set for yourself somewhere at all times.
Your business and your property is more
important than making friends or being
nice.

✓ Complete inventory schedule of the suite
and forward to the reservations department.
If it's your own suite, have a complete list of
all inventory and include that in the guest
information book or laminate and leave
inside the door of a kitchen cupboard.
This way, the guests are aware that you are
aware of all of the contents and can even
alert you if there are any items that are
missing that you missed when doing your
own inventory.

✓ Have the signed contract forwarded to the
reservations department. If you are doing
your own, have copies of all contracts ready
for guests in both print form and a PDF
format that you can email to the guests.
Have a data base or a secure system of
storing and keeping track of all contracts.

Guest Representative Manual

A guest service representative is an extremely important part of our company, and all steps must be followed in order to ensure our guests have an exceptional experience with our company.

The reservations department has worked very hard up until this point to make the reservation for the guest and prepare them for their trip to Vancouver. Your position is to welcome them to your city and answer any and all questions that they may have to ensure a comfortable stay. While communicating with us for months about their stay, you will be the very first person they get to meet face-to-face. There are several rules and policies in place to make sure the guests have a wonderful stay with us while at the same time maintaining the safety and security of the company.

The following is the procedure that must take place in order for the guests to have an excellent customer experience with us.

You will receive an email the evening before a guest's arrival with their information, such as name, the suite in which they are staying, and their approximate time of arrival. Had they made any special requests such as cots or cribs, extra towels, etc., this will be included in your email. This is emailed to you the evening before in case there are any items you need to take care of the evening prior or just to organize your day the next day. As you are contracted for the entire day, it is your responsibility to take care of all guests on your contracted day. You may give away your check-ins to another guest representative should you not be able to make it or want to make other plans. Regardless, it is the contractor's responsibility to make sure all guests are checked in in a timely fashion and without any delays.

You will also receive a confirmation email about 9 a.m. the day of your scheduled work day. Any last-minute changes, overnight emails, or voicemails that came in will be included in this email. The reservations department works hard at trying to get the guests' arrival information ahead of time so that you can schedule the guests' check-ins accordingly. A contact phone number will also be provided for the guest in case you would like to call them ahead of time with any questions you may have about their arrival. Keep in mind, each contractor may only use the company cell phones to contact each guest and may never at any time for any reason use their own personal phone to contact a guest.

A guest will call the company cell phone approximately an hour prior to arriving at their suite. We suggest this to the guests so that in case their flight or other travel arrangements are delayed, the guest will not need to worry about contacting us ahead of time to advise us. For the company, there would be no need for the guest representative to sit and wait for a guest whose flight has been delayed. This way, the guest is relieved of the stress that they will be late for their check-in and the guest representative is also not waiting needlessly for a guest when they could be checking in another guest.

Although the guest has been emailed these instructions as well as reminded prior to their departure from their homes, they have on occasion, forgotten to call and only call to advise that they are at the building.

During this phone call when they call an hour ahead of time, please be sure to ask how their travels were so far and how they are doing. See if they require any driving directions, and if they are driving, instruct them to park at the back of the building where the garage entrance is so that you can guide them to their parking stalls. If they are being dropped off, simply advise them where the front entrance is and if you will be waiting for them in the lobby to help them with their luggage or if they are to buzz into the suite and you will come down and assist them at that time. Always ask to see if there is anything else required for them prior to their arrival at the suite. This is not a phone call for your convenience so that you know how much longer you have to sit at Starbucks, but it is your first chance to impress the guests with your customer service skills. Always put yourself in their shoes and think of what would it take to impress you.

Should a guest call to advise they are onsite, simply let the guest know you have not received their prior phone call to advise that they are on their way, and advise them of how long it will take you to get to them. At no point ever should they be reminded that they had to call ahead with an hour notice and that it's somehow their fault. They could have already called and we just somehow missed their call, didn't get the message, or numerous other reasons. Always assume that it's our fault that we didn't get their message and that we will be there as soon as possible to check them in.

Arrive at the suite at least 15 minutes prior to their arrival and conduct the following steps:

1. Check to make sure that the entire suite is clean, all towels are accurate, beds look fantastic, and everything is working (phone, television, Internet, etc.)
2. Confirm that your iPod is working for checking in the guests. You will need to access your electronic sign-in sheet for the check-in form and ensure that your credit card machine is working properly.
3. Turn on the heat to an adequate room temperate, depending on the season. About 20 degrees is the average. You may also turn on the lights so that when the guests arrive, everything is ready for them. If you know there will be children coming, have the television already on a children's channel so that when the family gets to the suite, the kids can be occupied so that the parents can complete their check-in.

You should then wait for the guests either at the entrance of the garage gate or the lobby of the building, depending on how they will be arriving.

If the guests are driving themselves, please meet them at the entrance. Open the doors for them, wait for the gates to close, and proceed to have them follow you to their assigned parking stall. Assist them with parking should they require help. Offer to take their luggage and assist them in any way you can.

Should the guests arrive by taxi or limousine, please wait for them in the lobby and immediately help them with their luggage into the building and into their suites. While entering the building and elevators, show them how the fobs work as not every country has a fob system. We have witnessed one lady waiving her fob in front of the building doors, hoping the doors would magically open, without realizing that there is a certain spot the fob must touch in order for the door to open. Never assume, always show.

Allow the guests to go into the suite first, and once inside they can remove their shoes, and then you can assist them with their luggage into the suite. Ask where each piece of luggage goes, which ones go to the master bedroom and which ones go into the second bedroom. It's always nicer when your luggage is placed in the room that it belongs to. Not only is this less work on the guests, but you are going to make sure that the walls are not damaged as they drag their luggage around the corners and through the hallways.

Ask the guests for their credit card as well as photo identification. Prior to their arrival, the guests are made aware that they must produce their photo identification as well as their credit card. The name on the credit card MUST match the name on the photo identification. This name must also match the name of the person that the reservation is under. This would be the same name that has been provided to you on your email with your check-ins. There are no exceptions, and if they are missing one or the other, you are to call the reservations department immediately.

Complete a walk-through with the guests, as per the electronic check-in form, and take notes of any damage that is already in the suite. All other damage that is not noted on the check-in form will be the responsibility of the guest. Have the guests fill out the electronic sheet as per the instructions given.

As the guest representative, you are required to fill in your part of what suite you checked them into as well as what keys were given to the guest. Each and every single key must be accounted for. This includes an "F" for fob, a "K" for an actual key, "G" for a garage door opener, "M" for mailbox keys, etc. For example, for a set of keys that has a fob with two keys, you would write down, "1F/2K", meaning one fob and two keys.

Guests are NOT permitted to have mailbox keys unless they are staying with us for an extended period of time and you are asked by the reservations department to give them a set of mailbox keys. Mailbox keys are included with the housekeeper's keys, and these are separate from the guest's keys. Do NOT ever give a guest keys to the mailbox unless specifically asked to do so by the reservations department. If giving a guest mailbox keys without authorization, you will be responsible for any liabilities associated with giving out those keys without the prior written consent of the company.

Each set of keys must be written out separately. If there are two sets of identical keys, they will be written as, "1F/2K and 1F/2K" which means they have two sets of exactly the same keys.

Credit card authorization MUST be done every single time. The guest is made aware ahead of time that they will be required to have their credit card pre-authorized upon checking in. Although they have already paid for their reservation, we are still required to swipe their credit card to ensure that their card is valid. Unless it is stated in your check-in form from the reservations department that credit card authorization is not required, then you will be required to do one. Should a guest argue that they have already paid for their reservation, you will be required to explain to them that it's not for their payment; it is just to confirm that their credit card is valid. It is part of their contract that they signed and part of their agreement. Their agreement states that they will not receive the keys without a pre-authorization, whether or not their reservation has been paid for or not. Any questions at any time, please call the reservations department right away. It is important to note that:

No pre-authorization = No keys! NO EXCEPTIONS!

Should you give a guest keys to the suite without completing a proper pre-authorization, the following will result:

1. You will not be paid for the full check-in.

2. You will be liable for any damage to the suite or any other financial loss as a result of the guest obtaining keys to the suite without the authorization of the company.

Now that their identification has been checked, their credit card processed, and the electronic document completed, feel free to answer any questions that the guests have about their suite and the surrounding areas. They will be interested to know where the nearest 24-hour convenience store is as well as any other 24-hour food stores. Guest who are traveling from the other side of the world will experience jet lag and will probably be awake at 3 or 4 in the morning. It's nice to know where the nearest stores are. Also, give them some points of interest such as high-end restaurants, restaurants for the budget-conscious, shopping centers, transportation such as taxi or trains/buses, etc.

Ensure that the guests are aware how to access the parkade, where the garbage room is, where the Internet information is located, and how to contact the company. Make sure you are aware of all of the house rules so you can pass them along to the guests. Explain to them about the checkout procedure, that checkout time is 10 a.m. They are to leave all keys inside the suite on the kitchen table. They are to remove the front door key off the keychain, lock the door, and slide the key back under the door. They will be able to leave through the front lobby only. If they have a vehicle, they must remove the vehicle from the garage prior to locking the door and leaving the keys inside as they will not be able to get into the garage once the keys are left inside the suite.

All of our suites are non-smoking which also includes the balconies. Our guests will be fined $500 for smoking anywhere inside the suite, the balcony, or anywhere in the building. Most suites do not allow pets, and guests will also be fined $300 for every time we have found out that there were pets on the premises. Although you are not required to go over all of the rules with each guest, you must be familiar with all of them in case they have specific questions about them.

Once you have left the guest in their suite, please call the reservations department immediately after leaving to confirm that a guest has been checked in and if there is any follow-up that the reservations department is required to do with the guest.

Any questions at any time, please call the office immediately.

I hope that these checklists and sample manuals are enough to get you started and on your way to doubling your rental profits. Don't forget to focus on paying down your mortgage, saving some money along the way, and then preparing for your retirement. Once these systems are set up and running smoothly, your mortgage paid off, and you are retired, you will enjoy the fruits of your labor. Hopefully, we can meet up for together for that pina colada on the beach!

For further information, please visit us online at www. profitsinrealestaterentals.com or email us at:

info@profitsinrealestaterentals.com

If you are ever in the Vancouver area, please book a stay with us at www.luxurycorporatesuites.com

We look forward to having you stay with us!